From PREHISTORY *to the* PRESENT DAY

Fashion

THE Ultimate

History

OF Costume

STEFANELLA SPOSITO

promopress

Stefanella Sposito lives and works in Milan, where teaches Fashion History, History of Fabric and Textile Products in Italy's Sistema Moda state professional schools. She is the author of numerous critical essays and articles published in art and fashion magazines such as *Filoforme*, *Jacquard*, and *Moodmagazine.* She leads international seminars and conferences on fabric techniques and history and directs research in this field. Some of her work has been published by influential magazines such as *Vogue* Italia.

Fashion: The Ultimate History of Costume
From Prehistory to the Present

Original title:
Il racconto della moda
Dalla Preistoria ai nostri giorni

Translation: Kevin Krell

ISBN: 978-84-15967-82-8

Copyright © 2016 Ikon Editrice srl – Milan
1st edition, September 2016
Copyright © 2016 Promopress for the English edition

Promopress is a trademark of:
Promotora de prensa internacional S.A.
C/ Ausiàs March 124
08013 Barcelona, Spain
Tel.: 0034 932451464
Fax: 0034 932654883
Email: info@promopress.es
www.promopresseditions.com
Facebook: Promopress Editions
Twitter: Promopress Editions @PromopressEd

First English edition: 2016

Design: spread: David Lorente with the collaboration of Claudia Parra

Printed in China

TABLE OF CONTENTS

CREDITS AND ACKNOWLEDGMENT

PHOTOS
Federico Garolla: 188, 190, 191, 192, 193,
194, 196, 197, 198, 200, 201,205, 206, 225

Johnny Moncada: 202, 211, 212, 213

Dominique Fradin: 215

Patrizia Savarese: 221

Indigitalitalia: 237, 238, 239, 241, 245, 246, 247, 248,249,
250 251, 252, 253, 256

Archivio Storico dell'Arte (A.S.A.), Milan
for the photographs of pictoral works on pages 64 to 164

ILLUSTRATIONS
Silvia Segalini : 6, 11, 12, 13, 20, 22, 24, 25, 29, 34, 38,
39, 40, 68, 70, 74, 80, 84, 96, 100, 102, 104, 106, 108,113,
118, 122, 128, 150, 156, 164, 170, 177, 179, 184, 185, 199,
204, 208, 210, 215, 220, 229, 230, 241, 245

Setarium, Educational Museum of Silk, Como
226, 227, 242, 243, 244, 245

Manuela Brambatti
234, 235, 238, 240

Civiche Raccolte Stampe Bertarelli, Milan
Etchings and historical photographs

Uncredited photographs and images
Archivio Grafica&Disegno
Collection of the author

Special and warm thanks to:
- Valentina Moncada
- Isabella Garolla
for authorsing use of the archive photographic
archived of her legendary progenitors

INTRODUCTION

The form, details and colours of a garment reflect, more than anything, the ideological idiosyncrasies of people and are intimately connected to the behaviours that express the society in which we live. They contribute to creating an overall atmosphere, the "mirror of an age", which characterises the psychology of the times. The idea of pointless, superficial fashion, at times an expression of affectation, that exists as an end itself is ultimately overcome. Despite the old saying, "The habit doesn't make the monk", we all grant a significant role to clothing. The Latin word "habitus" can be inter-prered, first and foremost, as "external appearance" and, more generically, as "behaviour". The search for elegance, an expressive form associated with improving one's own appearance, dates back to the time when humans began to abandon nudity, reflecting the longings of their collective imagination as well as the depth of their inner selves. How can we deny that a pair of gloves, a hat, a shawl or a piece of jewellery is capable of highlighting the personality of the person that wears them, adding or emphasising charm, mystery, security, belonging, empathy, attraction or repulsion (and much more) in our relationships with others?

To narrate the evolution of clothes and their preferred accessories is to set out on a complex, rich and multi-faceted journey that impacts and permeates social, religious, psychological, economic and stylistic constructs of extreme importance. It is almost impossible to separate clothing from historical circumstances, because fashion manifests itself as a direct rep-resentation of events and often is highly conditioned by them. Aesthetic elements determine authentic and personal "body styles". They define the form and general appearance of garments and contribute to determining the structure of the clothes that we wear.

Through a myriad sequence of variables opportunely combined with one other, highlighting different anatomical features, the body reveals or conceals, is exalted or mortified, offers or refuses to be seen, invites or shuns desire, judgment, interpretation and wonder. The objective of this book is to stimulate a certain curiosity surrounding these matters, guiding the reader in the discovery of unexpressed thoughts, explicit messages and symbols that clothes contain and continue to express beyond their mere functionality.

It is undoubtable that fashion also reaffirms specific moral values: opu-lence, ostentation, dissipation, modesty, reserve, austerity, power, conformity and provocation, to name just a few. We should be aware of the extent to which our personal style of dress or how we wear a garment, as a genuine and characteristic means of support, can influence this. Observing public personalities that are exposed to the media, we notice how skillfully they manipulate the expressive potential of clothes and manage it in a precise and studied way (or at least someone does for them). In reality, ordinary people also utilise the communicative power of clothing, adapting it to the needs, occasions for use and conventions that interest them most. We do not dress simply to cover ourselves with the most available raw materials in our country. While nowadays some of us we would like to see a return to more honest and ethical behaviour, the globalisation of goods and con-sumption is an indication of the footprint of modern times. In a society so imbued with virtual pollution as ours, the value of iconic representation is immense. This ambiguous game between being and seeming to be is practically a basic necessity. And what is more fundamental than clothes, which since time immemorial have had the ability to merge with the per-son who wears them?

Peoples of antiquity

PRE-HISTORIC CLOTHING

The first references to fabrics date back to 9000 B.C. in Shanidar (Iraq). Other archaeological remains date back to 7000-6000 B.C. in Jarmo (Iraq) and Çatal Hüyük (Turkey) and are an indication of the urgent need of ancient human beings to protect their body from the elements and the dangers and adverse situations to which they were constantly exposed. The hunting-gathering activities in the natural environment provided the stones, husks, seeds, berries, bird feathers, shells, teeth and animal claws used to fashion necklaces and amulets, constituting the first known instances of adornment.

Ochre and earth-toned body paint, scarifications, tattoos and scares superimposed on the skin and exhibited with pride, as they often had been obtained through arduous contests of bravery that fortified the spirit and gained the favour of the gods, had the same protective function.

The first garments were made of hides and skins which, after tanning and softening were punctured with stone punches and sewn with animal tendons. Wearing their hunting trophies, cavemen exhibited their supremacy over animals. Appropriating the scalps and skins of wild boars, they made their prey's ferocity, strength, astuteness and sharp reflexes their own, endowing them with a sense of invincibility in the face of any enemy. The decorative stitching reinforing the seams of the textile surface inscribed on the fabric a silent code of signs of acknowledgment which was transferred from the body to clothing.

Pre-historic archaelogical discoveries indicate the use of fibres prepared with marsh plants, flexible herbaceous plants and threads from tree bark (lime trees, weeping willows, birches) that were softened in water and joined and twisted with the fingers. Wild

Cro-Magnon artists, France, painting in Font-de-Gaume, Charles R. Knight, 1920

linen was very widespread because of its tensile strength and was also used to make string. Goat, reindeer and deer hairs were used to weave thread nets, braids and spiral wraps that date back to the Upper Paleolithic Era in Europe (Lascaux cave, France; Tassili n'Ajjer, western Sahara) and were used to make mats, everyday instruments, sandals and caps.

Netting, a basic fabric that also was made with nettles, has multiple applications in rigid or soft form. The Sprang technique allowed for making reticular structures on a small stick loom.

The reconstruction of the appearance of clothing in this period is based on cave paintings in Spain and statuettes of gods. Some images depict men in pants and boots while women are wearing skirts and wide garments, an interpretation confirmed by the discovery of small needles of bone with an eyehole that were used to sew clothes. The Tarim mummy and Similaun Man, nicknamed "the iceman", wore leather loincloths and leather footwear that covered the thighs and calves. Prehistoric humans, in addittion, wore a cloak formed by lenghts of light – and dark – coloured strips of goat skin, sewn with animal tendons and cinched with a long belt with a pouch that was looped twice around and then knotted at the waist. Prehistoric man wore a bearskin cap and intricate

Prehistoric leather pouch

footwear consisting of an inner and outer shoe. A mat-like cape made from grass plants protected him from the elements.

In addition to preparation of diverse plant fibres, a technique for producing felt was adopted to obtain a compact, warm and comfortable textile surface. Felt was obtained by carding wads of dampened wool that were sprinkled with animal fat and fulled to obtain sheets. Felt was used above all for caps and footwear, but also tents and huts. Textile technique evolved slowly. In the Upper Neolithic Era (4500-3300 B.C.) and in the Age of Metals, different processes were used to weave not only satchels and saddlebags but capes, tunics and belts as well. The first rudimentary looms appeared. These functioned thanks to a system of rods and cords, and were used to make fabrics whose borders already had edges. The development of fabrics furthered the spread of hemp and wool. Experimentation extended to diagonal structures and square, chevron and rhombus patterns when heddles became an integral part of the loom and work instruments were perfected.

Nordic peoples wore an elliptical or rectangular cape that swaddled them completely like a blanket and was fastened at the breast with a brooch. Examples of this type of garment were discovered in Scandanavia in fifty sepulchres, made with tree trunks, containing the remains of people that had lived during the Bronze Age. The cape was not cut but woven with the desired length to highlight the edges and frayed borders. The Thorsberg cloak, which was discovered in Jutland and dates back to the Iron Age (2000 B.C.), and which was reconstructed from seven pieces of wool, possesses similar characteristics.

Below: Borum Eshoj, cap, Denmark
Right: Prehistoric clothes

Another interesting discovery was a pair of pants in eastern Frisia made from a single piece of fabric in which the two sides were folded towards the centre. As burial mounds in Borum Eshoj and Egtved, in Denmark (1370 B.C.), attest to, women's clothing consisted of a skirt-apron formed by a series of cords and attached at the waist with a wool belt buckled with a large bronze disk with spiral decorations. A corset with elbow-length sleeves girded women's breasts, or they were covered by a V-neck blouse with kimono sleeves. Women also wore bronze cuffs around their wrists.

SUMERIANS

As the origin of the name *shumer* ("cultivated land") suggests, the Sumerians are considered the first sedentary population to settle in Lower Mesopotamia. The Sumerians lived from hunting and farming. Important technical and demographic transformations made possible the organisation of life around the independent city-states of Ur, Uruk, Nippur and Lagash, equipped with an efficient political and military system that managed the economy and established precise codes of behaviour, resulting in a class-based society. The vast number of votive estatuettes found suggests a fervent spiritual life in which all the important activities of the community were concentrated in the ziggurat, or temple-palace.

In the bas-relief of Ur Nina (3000 B.C.), the figures are wearing kaunakes, skirts adorned with fleeces arranged as superimposed borders, similar to flounces. The fleeces have a wave-like movement that emulates a head of hair. Long-hair wool fabrics were preferred by all strata of society, to the point where sometimes the garments are confused with the hair of ewes and rams, arranged and painted in a highly realistic mannner. Military attire was similar to civilian dress. The priest-king, who is wearing a circular diadem, has long, wavy hair gathered at the back of the neck in a bun and small, loose curls on sides of the face.

A distinctive feature of the Sumerians was a meticulously cared for beard, which hangs long and square over the throat and

Alabaster statue of Ebih II

Punched relief that represents King Ur-Nanshe

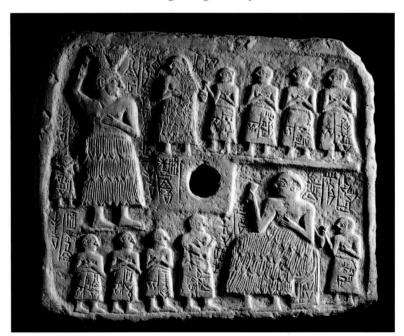

consists of compact ring-like curls similar to a necklace. Headwear in the form of a cap or turban were common in men and women. Queens and priests adopted heavy layers of tresses that covered the shoulders and were open in front or arranged asymmetrically.

Women's hair resembled compact wigs. Its shape and volume, obtained with the help of hairpieces, were noteworthy. The gold and silver objects found in the tomb of the Sumerian princess Puabi (3000 B.C.) – gold cuffs and earrings, lapis lazuli and cornaline necklaces – are also worth noting. The sovereign wore an elaborate headpiece adorned with rows of poplar leaves made out of fine sheets of gold and embossed gold flowers sprinkled with lapis lazuli.

ASSYRIANS AND BABYLONIANS

From the second millenium B.C. on, two groups of people of Semitic origin inhabited the area between the Tigris and Eufrates Rivers: the Assyrians (northern part) and the Babylonians (center-south).

THE STANDARD OF UR

The Standard of Ur (2700-2500 B.C.), preserved in the British Museum in London, depicts battle scenes with the capture of the enemy. Men and women are wrapped in skirts or cloaks made with fleece fabrics or long fringes, arranged in rings, which, in the absence of more concrete documentary sources, we can assume were probably made of goat or ram's hair.

Assyrian-Babylonian statuettes and bas reliefs

Written testimonies from both peoples are inscribed in cuneiform characters carved on clay tablets. According to the archaeologist Bayet, these people "were fond of reproducing scenes from daily life and the increasing use of clothes and embroidered fabrics, an indication of the spread of a sophisticated culture that came from the orient."

The reliefs of stone funeral steles and marble plaques and seals bear witness to the fact that despite living in a warm climate, the Assyrians and Babylonians covered themselves with heavy fabrics, densely decorated and adorned with tassels, trim and embossed gold rosettes.

The sovereign, a brave and commanding male figure, always dressed sumptuously, whether embarking on a lion hunt in a chariot or during official ceremonies during which he offered libations and sacrifices to the gods. The dress style was Asian, and there were no substantial sartorial differences between the sexes. Both men and women wore the kandis, a long, brightly coloured tunic with short sleeves. On top of this garment they wore a shawl with fringes wrapped in a spiral around the body like an apron and held in a place by a long band of fabric. A strap crossed in the front held a quiver filled with arrows on the back. The girded line of the garments evidences exact reproductions of textile decorations: circles, rosettes, checkerboards and horizontal bands that adorned formal royal clothing. The attire of priests and eunuchs was the same and matched the royal frocks. This type of shawl was highly valued in Rome. In the literary work Satyricon, reference is made to the splendour of Assyrian-Babylonian dyes, comparing them to the multi-coloured feathers of a peacock. The Assyrian and Babylonian peoples paid special attention to their curly black hair. They also took meticulous care of their beards, which they combed in African braids arranged in orderly rows. For footwear, they wore flat-soled sandals elevated in the back, with a transverse strap through the big toe which tied at the ankle.

Egyptian path of souls

Relief from the Ptolemic period

EGYPTIANS

Egyptian culture, documented by hieroglyphic sources, flourished on the banks of the Nile River, a narrow portion of land between the Mediterranean and Red Sea, growing flax and building grandiose pyramids that functioned as tombs for the absolute monarchs of the thirty-one dynasties that succeeded one another in power beginning in 3000 B.C. Religious spirituality influenced Egyptian clothing, which was perfectly adapted to the arid and warm climate of the enclave. Apparel was always the same length, and only the size of the different accessories varied.

The *kalasiris*, a broad flax tunic with pleats, clung to the body, providing freedom of movement. Formed by a single piece of fabric folded in half and with a central opening, it passed over the shoulder, fell in accordian pleats and was knotted below the chest. Burial frescoes evidence the mastery of artisans who were experts in fabrics, pleating and gold work. Cloths were plant-based because wool was considered impure. White was the predominant colour, with infrequent blue or red stripes. The fabric, similar to gauze, was so delicate and airy that the knee- or ankle-length tunics could be worn on top of each other.

Bearers of gifts adopted the use of narrow tunics with a girdle held in place with long straps that sometimes revealed the naked chest. They were profusely decorated in manifold ways with interwoven coloured bead snoods or with tesseras of dyed leather. Upper class men preferred the *schenti*, a short, pleated kilt fastened to the sides with a polychrome belt from which hung a rigid triangular panel made with enamel applications, glazed paste and filigree gold. Servants, workers and the popular classess wore simple loincloths and left their bare torso. The claft, a striped headdress similar to that of the sphinxes worn over the forehead and knotted at the back of the neck, protected the head.

Women wore enormous black wigs. They went barefoot or wore light beach-like sandals with an arched toe that were woven with

papyrus or palm fibres. The combination of magnificent amulets and carved beetles, highly symbolic of protection, and naturalistic ornaments such as garlands of gold lotus leaves (divine material that radiated light) contributed to articulating the hierarchy that governed the organisation of work in Egyptian society. The Egyptian people paid special attention to cosmetics and frequently used ochre and red-earth and unguent perfumes, which were sprayed on the body from which the hair had been removed. Both sexes outlined the eyes with a greasy black line that gave them a more elongated look similar to the eyes of a cat, an animal venerated in Egypt. The eyelids were brushed with turquoise powders.

From left to right: Nefertari and guardian statue from the time of Tutankhamun

EGYPTIAN JEWELLERY

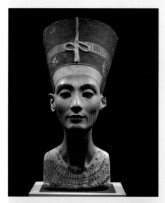

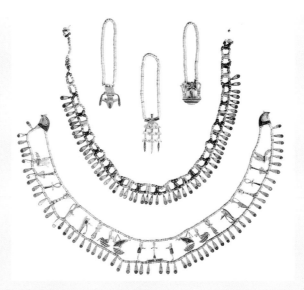

Jewellery of Princess Khnumit, c. 1750 B. C.
Cairo, Egyptian Museum

Refined gold and silver objects expressed Egyptian magical-religious values and indicated the owner's social status. The king gave pieces of jewellery to his subjects as a reward for their merits or jewellery was donated to the temple in the form of ceremonial offerings.
The Egyptians believed that funerary objects guaranteed protection for the part of the deceased person's body on which it was worn.
They wore wrist and ankle bracelets, rigid circular cuffs around the arms and the *shebyu*, grain or glazed majolica necklaces, around their necks. A honeycombed gold breast-plate representing a sun falcon with its wings spread evoked the embrace of the divinity and was placed on the pharoh's mummy, while a necklace of the "flies of gold" was awarded to military officials who had distinguished themselves on the field of battle. Men and women both wore the *hosch*, an imposing flat necklace of several rows knotted in the back and finished off with a pendant which adhered seamlessly and ended in a small cape.

Amenhotep III

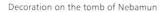

Decoration on the tomb of Nebamun

HEBREWS

The pride of belonging to their particular religious community defines the history of the Hebrews in their choice of clothing as well. Information about what the ancient Hebrews wore comes from biblical texts, which embody the symbolic nature that characterises every aspect of life of the Hebrew people, who were orginally from Chaldea and arrived in Palestine around 2000 B.C. During the period of the bondage in Egypt, the "children of Israel" did not adopt their masters' manner of dress and preserved their identity completely. In fact, it is told that the young Moses was recognised as a Hebrew because of his clothes. Hebrew dress, which remained nearly unchanged for centuries, was identical for men and woman. The tunic and cap were basic garments, and variations were limited to colours, fabrics and manner of production. The Hebrews were also familiar with fine linen.

The use of garments made with a combination of linen or cotton and wool was strictly prohibited, as were mixed fabrics, in memory of the fratricide committed by Cain (a farmer) against Abel (a shepherd) that was motivated by God's acceptance of Abel's offering of the fruits of his labour and rejection of Cain's (Gen 4.1 - 16). Men wore a blue shirt embroidered with geometric designs and undergarments similar to a loincloth next to the skin. The tunic worn by men was white, straight and shorter than the one worn by women, which went down to their ankles. It had long sleeves and a series of vertical stripes finished with pendants. The inner edges of the collar could be embroidered with motifs that indicated one's region or town of origin. A knotted cord girded the waist, in keeping with the custom of separating the upper part of the body (seat of the heart and higher feelings) from the lower part (where human instincts reside).

Fresco of Moses in the river

Fresco of a man

The wealthiest men wore a kaftan, a tunic with short sleeves that reached down to the calf. In cold regions, the body was wrapped in a heavy woolen fabric, the *sindon*, which served as a cape or cloak and was made with two cuts to allow movement of the arms. On the edges of the cloak, the Pharisees wore blue strips to publicly demonstrate their observance of the Law. Prophets and Nazarenes wore simple cloaks made from animal skins. The Sephardim wore the *talit*, a wool shawl. The king wore the *aderet*, a richly ornamented robe.

They also wore sandals with leather soles and straps knotted at the calf. The disciples of Christ used sandals with a cord arranged in rings that were interlaced above the foot (Mc 6,9).

Footwear and capes were optional for the poor. Some religious rites proscribed cutting the hair regularly, and, consequently, men had long thick hair and abundant beards. The female tunic, often blue, had a V-neck with large embroidered edges. Below the tunic, women worn the *petigil*, a breastplate to support the breasts, and embroidered pants that reached the knee. A kaftan with sleeves so ample they nearly brushed the groud was worn on top of the tunic. A band that created elaborate pleats and gentle waves attached the kaftan to the waist. Fringes were commonly used as decoration. A rectangular scarf knotted with an interwoven drawstring covered the head. Unmarried women concealed their face under a veil as a sign of modesty (Gn 24,65). On their feet, they wore leather sandals made with a strip that passed between the big toe and second toe and then wrapped around the ankle (Lc 3,16).

Women also wore a cloak: a loose-fitting *mitpamat* which also covered the head. In the time of King David, the Hebrews' physical appearance became more magnificent, ultimately resulting in the unbridled luxury of the reign of Salomon. Women scented themselves with essence of myrrh and incense perfume and painted their lips. Men also wore jewellery, seal rings or different types of amulets.

RELIGIOUS ATTIRE

During solemn events, the high priest wore specific attire when performing the ritual sacrifice: a long tunic that reached the feet and a shorter one with long sleeves adorned with little gold bells. The *ephod*, a short apron-like garment of embroidered linen consisting of two rectangular panels tied with straps and embellished with ribbons and fringes, completed the priestly attire. A sash or belt called an *abnet* was tied around the waist. The ephod had a pouch decorated with jewels that held two dice, *urim* and *tummim*, which the priest rolled to learn the will of God. The breastplate, or *hoschen*, had twelve stones on which the name of God and the twelve tribes of Israel were engraved. The priest's headdress was a special turban in the form of a mitre.

PHOENICIANS

The eastern Mediterranean was populated by Phoenicians, Hitties and Chipriots. Since the Homeric Age, the Phoenician cities of Byblos, Sidon and Tyre were considered major extraction and distribution centres of murex, a pigment obtained from mollusks used to make an indelible dye of different red and violet hues.

Expert seafarers, the Phoenicians possessed powerful fleets and, because they had also mastered dyeing techniques, traded extensively in fabrics and dyes, transforming murex juice into one of the most expensive and highly appreciated products throughout the Mediterranean region. Twelve thousand shells were needed to obtain 1.5 grams of pigment, in addition to a complex preparation process for dyeing a cut of cloth, which limited its consumption to the privileged classes.

Murex brandaris shells

Left: *Youth of Mozia*, Sicily

Phoenecian jewellery

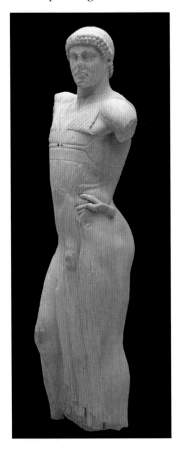

Desired by Macedonians, Romans, Etruscans and Byzantines and valued in many oriental courts, murex became synonymous with refinement and wealth, an emblem of political and religious power throughout the known world. A strongly trade-oriented livelihood, nurtured through continuous contact with foreign lands, was not conducive to the emergence of original expressive features in art and manner of dress, which consisted of a linen or wool tunic with a wide collar sewn with soft folds and was loose at the waist thanks to a belt. The Phoenecians also wore short skirts of Egyptian inspiration and wide cloaks or close-fitting tunics that fell to the knee. Initially, Phoenician attire imitated the Egyptian style of dress and, later, that of the Aegeans.

The same cultural influence is found in amulets, masks and artisanal objects, bearing witness to technical skills in the production of glass and metals. For adornment, the Phoenecians wore Pâte de verre jewellery formed by heads that alternated with rods decorated in relief. They often wore, as pendants, little glass bottles that contained perfumed essences, cross-shaped earrings and gold filigree or embossed gold necklaces.

All Phoenicians wore sandals that attached to the feet with coloured straps. The use of stiff rectangular or conical hats, worn in ceremonial rites honouring the goddess Astarte, was important, in particular the *lebbade*, a simple felt had attached under the chin with a leather strap. Meanwhile, the women, patiently awaiting the men's return from sea, wore simple diadems on the forehead to support bangs that fell to their shoulders. Some statuettes represent the *sarmat*, a headdress formed by a pyramidal mitre with a decorated band on the forehead, dangling earrings, two very large side disks at the height of the ears and a gold chain with a charm on the chest.

Bas-relief. Archaeological site of Yazılıkaya (Turkey)

Between 1650 and 1600 B.C., the first Hittite state emerged in Anatolia under the protectorate of the city of Kutelpe and inherited all the technologies known in the Neolithic Period.

Experts in raising horses, about which they wrote a manual dating back to 1400-1300 B.C., the Hittites were adept riders and builders of two-wheel carts. The production quality of the iron tools they used was exceptional. They were familiar with etching, embossing, crimping and modeling of metals forged in simple, geometrical shapes. During the Bronze Age, they perfected and disseminated this technique throughout Asia Minor and Mesopotamia, ultimately assuming an important role in the international political and military panorama. A warrior people of Indo-European origin, the Hittites established their first capital in Nesa, a city sufficiently rich to boast a zoo, and, later, in Hattusa, situated to the east of Ankara.

In Yazilikaya, a prehistoric temple from the 13th century B.C., is a sculpted figure of King Tudhaliya (1250-1220 B.C.) wearing a long cloak and a cap.

Another scene depicts the encounter between Teshub, god of sky and storm, and Hebat, the sun goddess. Hebat is clad in a long tunic with bat-like sleeves tightened at the waist with a band that forms pleats and a tall cylindrical cap atop loose hair, while Teshub is wearing a conical tiara with decorated motifs in relief. In another image, on the Gate of Hattusa, the same god is represented with a nude torso and a short skirt that reveals the legs. A helmet with horns encircles his head. The sculpure highlights the musculature of the legs and the hair on the god's chest, placing emphasis on masculine attributes in a mytho-religious sense. On the island of Cyprus, the Hittites worked with copper and marble and were continuously combining local elements with Anatolian, Mycenaean, Phonecian and Egyptian influences.

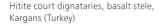

Hitite court dignataries, basalt stele, Kargans (Turkey)

PERSIANS

The legacy of the civilisations of Asia Minor was preserved in Achaemenid Persia, which, between the 6th and 4th centuries B.C (550-331), encompassed Egypt and Iran, extended to the Oxus regions and occupied part of the provinces of Punjab and Sindh.

The Persians, a mountain people that originated in current-day Turkistan, widely respected the uses and attire of the people living under their occupation and assimilated their ideas.

Susa and Persepolis are cities with a scenographic appearance, with imposing architectural constructions and series of stylised decorations. During this time, the oldest surviving knotted rug was woven employing Persian production techniques in the 5th century B.C. and discovered in a tomb on the Siberian steppe. It is made of wool, is square and predominatly red with a five-strip border. Among the decorations are squares with stars, stylised mythological creatures, reindeer and horses.

The Persians adopted a base layer tunic over which they wore a decorated *kandis*. Taken from the Assyrians, the kandis was a garment with wide, bell-shaped sleeves (characterised by a cone-shaped fabric insert) that opened fan-like from the elbow down.

Persian footwear consisted of soft triple-tie slippers. Types of headdress were the *bashliq*, a conical hood with a hanging tassel, with or without a band that covered the ears, a puffed cap or a rigid tiara of corrugated metal.

The powerful Persian army united solidiers of diverse ethnicities: Medes, Assyrians, Colchians, Thracians, Ethiopians and Arabs, noteworthy for their multi-coloured attire. The military uniform adopted the dress style of the nobility: a knee-length inner tunic to facilitate movement. Under the tunic, the valiant Persian soldiers wore the *anaxyrides*, the first pants prototype in antiquity (these would later evolve into modern pants), and comfortable cloth slippers that were replaced in battle with high leather boots. When engaged in war, Persian fighters were equipped with metal armour, leather pants, bow and arrows, a dagger hanging from the belt and a wicker shield. Little has been documented regarding the clothing worn by Persian women. Two female figures, depicted on another rug, wear ornate tunics similar to those used by archers, probably worn over a base layer tunic, and ankle boots with heels. The use of a veil, which descended straight down the back from a tiara, appears to have been obligatory in order to preserve a woman's virtue.

FORMAL DRESS

The long, flowing gala dress that the king and his entourage used for ceremonies was also worn by the Medes and characterised by extensive draping fabric.

The most significant illustration appears on an enamel terracota frieze in the palace of Darius in Susa (4th century B.C.). It depicts a procession of immortals, archers of the royal guard, armed with quivers and spears. While the attire is military, the garments consist of light fabric decorated with small, motley geometric motifs. The beautiful edges are arranged in stylised series of yellow, blue, ochre and brown.

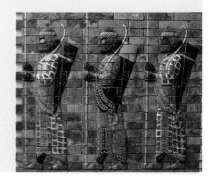

Plate. Persian archer

Persian helmet

Achaemenid period relief, Persepolis

Right: *Pazyryk* carpet from Altai

Persian plate

CRETANS

In 3000 B.C., a flourishing independent civilisation emerged that was distinguished by its peaceful and leisurely lifestyle.

The Cretans practiced a variety of sports, which contributed to their maintaining a slim and attractive figure, and organised parties, shows, contests and religious ceremonis. The bull and the snake were totemic animals considered to be divine.

The style of dress of Cretan women, reproduced in seals, statuettes and mural frescoes, was highly original for the time, very close-fitting in the upper part, suggesting the existence of a sophisticated cutting and sewing tradition.

Cretan women were considered the most elegant in the Mediterranean world. The dress worn by the snake goddess has a wide neckline that underscores the prominence of the breasts and leaves the stomach flat, cinching the waist in a rigid corset with short, narrow sleeves that cause the shoulders, drawn back, to arch. A curved apron covers the sides. The hourglass shape is achieved with a wide ruffled skirt, adorned with geometric embroidery, that opens downwards like a bell.

The Aegean people were fond of bright dyes, especially yellow, blue and red. The most commonly used fibres were wool and linen, which were either wild or cultivated locally.

Spinning and weaving were feminine activities that made possible the production of fifty-centimetre fabric strips with chevron, zigzag or spiral motifs. In addition to material used to make clothes, they also weaved blankets, curtains, rugs and other accessories for the home. Fullers and dyers began to work on the island, raising mollusks to extract murex. Frescos from the palace of Knossos and the palace of Festo show details of hair gathered in gentle waves intertwined with strings of pearls.

The men's clothing that appears in the fresco of the Prince and the Lilies (1550 B.C.) consists of an elegant, very short loincloth-skirt fastened with a narrow belt that serves as a corset and cinches the waist. A tiara of lilies finished with peacock feathers holds the long hair, divided into undulating strands, in place.

The representations of funeral corteges with women bearing offerings and wearing spun and sewn garments are from the Hagia Triada sarcophagus and the mural painting from Tirinto. The flared inner tunic consisted of bright colours and ornamented edges. It was worn without a belt, was unisex and was used primarily for religious ceremonies. The Cretans wore sandals tied at the ankle, leather footwear or ankle boots. Cosmetics also played an important role in their lives, and perfume and ointment makers were common throughout Cretan society.

La Parisienne, Knossos, either a goddess or a priestess, has scarlet lips and eyes delineated with a black line to widen her gaze and make it more magnetic. Men depilated their chests regularly and anointed themselves with essential oils. The production of necklaces, bracelets and gold and copper pendants also contributed to the construction of a carefully honed image.

La Parisienne, Knossos

Minoan snake goddess, majolica

Right: Minoan fresco of the *Prince of the Lilies*

Cretan fresco

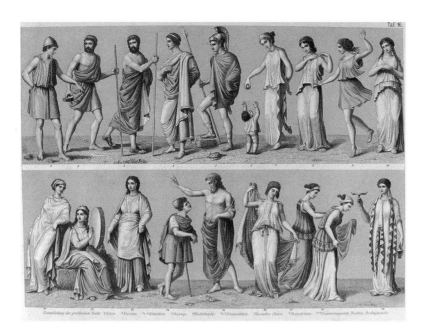

ANCIENT GREECE

Greek ideals, expressed in a community life characterised by debate, embraced dialogue as the method of seeking and discovering the truth. Within this cultutral framework emerged the foundations of modern Western thought: philosophy, oratory, politics, mythology, education, grammar, epic narrative, lyric poetry and theatre (tragedy and comedy).

The study of the spatial perception of the human anatomy, in particular, was applied to the fields of art and architecture. Images of women engaged in spinning and sewing, activities for which the matriarch of the house and her servants were responsible, appear frequently in the paintings that adorn the vessels of ancient Greece. In addition, women managed the family property and were personally responsible for ensuring that her family had clothes.

Depictions of looms show scenes of many women working together as a team on the same loom. The goddess Athena protected cloth, considered, like embroidery, a symbol of laboriousness and reflection. According to a legend, the technique of weaving derived from Arachne, daughter of Idmon, a dyer from Colophon, who had the temerity to challenge the goddess to a contest of skill in the art of weaving.

CHITON

The chiton, worn by Cretan women in the 6th century B.C., consisted of two sumperimposed linen rectangles (*pteryges*) sewn vertically to form a tube and briefly stitched at two points on the shoulders, thereby leaving three openings for the head and arms. The measurement of the cloth determined the tunic's form (narrow or wider) and the movement of the draped fabric, given that the pleats were elegantly distributed to form a pocket (*colpos*) with the help of a belt. On a wide chiton, the excess cloth falls down the length of the arm and is closed with a variety of brooches, creating a long-sleeve effect.

Inventors of the Olympics, the Greeks paid special attention to the harmony and beauty of the body through physical exercise, practiced in the arena, and displayed nudity without any false modesty. The headless Victory of Samothrace (preserved in the Louvre, in Paris) is the sculpture that best represents the Greeks' elaborate style of dress. Ancient Greeks, who believed that man is the measure of all things, erected temples with fluted columns and wore clothing full of pleats and undulations that granted a natural elegance to their gait and movements. From the Odyssey and other Latin literary works, we know that the ancient Greeks were very fond of intense colours and that their garments were not only white, as the majority of marble statues that we can see today would lead us to believe.

The most commonly used fibres were wool and linen. In the Hellenic period, the use of silk, often dyed before spinning, was adopted. Hemp and marine silk, obtained from a bivalve mollusk from the depths of the Mediterranean, were also used.

The art of dyeing was practiced in workshops through immersion in dye made with murex, kermes, oricello, garanza, saffron, indigo, safflower and white indigoberry plants, which were also combined to produce different tones.

Endowed with a deep artistic sensibility, the ancient Greeks named clothes according to their colours and tones: *melinon* was an apple-green garment, *batrachis* was frog green, *omphalion* was leek green and *aerinon* sky blue.

A rich archaelogical heritage provides numerous examples of clothing, which evolved in parallel with Greek art and architecture. The first archaic forms (700-500 B. C.) – in which women's attire was tightfitting and decorated with borders and geometric bands while men wore wool tunics with flowing pleats – gave way to the fashion of the classical age (500-323 B.C.), which was more linear and full, noteworthy for its tight pleats, chiaroscuro effects and the absence of embroidery. In the Hellenistic period (323-31 B.C.), the forms of garments became more opulent and the draping was flowing and excessively ornate, in fabrics that were always very light and colourful, indicating the decline of the fashion. Some of the essential elements of Greek clothing were common in men and women. Greek women wore the *peplo*, a heavy woolen garment, or the lighter linen chiton. Over this they wore the *himation*, a quadrangular cloak that protected the shoulders and the back and, at times, covered the face. On ancient coins we can observe whimsical coiffures in which the hair, curled with an iron, is gathered into smooth buns. Ringlets were tied with ribbons and collected with cloth tiaras and crowns. Sandals and buskins were the typical women's footwear.

Accessories included a breast-band called the *strophion* and a leaf-shaped fan. Men, active in civic life, also wore the chiton and himation. The masculine version of the chiton defined a man's importance in the community and his role in public life: "Know thyself first, and then dress accordingly," stated the philosopher Epictetus of Hierapolis (c. 50-125/130 A.D.). The chiton, which

extended to the feet and did not have a belt *(poderes)*, conferred a certain prestige to the elderly, priests and nobles. The oracles (such as the Delphic oracles) wore the chiton cinched at the waist to lead the chariot races, with a strap in the armpit that created a short sleeve. Tragic actors, zither players and singers also wore the long version of the chiton. The gods of Olympus wore it, too, except for Hermes, who, since he was a traveler, is distinguished by his short dress, pouch, sandals, winged cap and caduceus, or herald's staff, a symbol of commerce. The knee-length chiton was the daily attire of soldiers, artisans, workers and slaves. It consisted of the exomis, a rudimentary garment of coarse fabric held in place on one shoulder, similar to the one that the Amazons wore.

The agile body of Theseus, depicted in the fight against the Minotaur, was wrapped in a tunic – similar to that of other young heroes – that revealed the legs. The two models of chiton could be held in place on both shoulders *(amphimaschalos)* or on one shoulder *(eteromaschalos)*. The most common apparel worn on the upper part of the body was the himation and the *chlamys*.

There were two types of men's shoes: footwear that covered the feet completely *(embades, endromides,* buskins) with leather ankle boots of different heights or sandals with laces that formed a grid and joined to the foot with different fastenings *(crepidas* and *blautai)*. Thanks to their relations with Thryacia (northern Greece), Lydia and Scylla (southern Russia), the Greeks were exposed to the influence of exotic and barbarous fashions, incorporating foreign customs into their garment making.

THE CHLAMYS

A short, wool cloak used in the military. The chalmys originated in Thessaly. It was held in place on the left shoulder or the chest to facilitate movement of the arms. It became a symbol of virility, worn by young men between the ages of eighteen and twenty or travelers, who wore the chalmys combined with the *petaso*, a wide-brimmed hat. Artisans and sailors were distinguished by the *pilos*, a conical hat.

Head of Meneleus

THE HIMATION

The himation fell symetrically on the shoulder and rested on the arms. It was held in place asymmetrically with a brooch or was wrapped around the body completely. This latter version, called the *tribonion*, was suitable for philosophers and orators who made eloquent gestures and concealed their right arm beneath the cloak. In some cases, the himation substituted the chiton and wrapped around the naked male body completely, leaving the right arm free.

MILITARY ATTIRE

The Hellenic army was made up of citizen-warriors equipped with a helmet, armour and leggings and armed with a spear and circular shield *(hoplon)*. Some scenes painted on vessels depict the rite of dressing of the hoplites, Hellenic citizens-soldiers skilled in fighting in the phalanx formation of military combat. The Amazons, legendary women warriors, are sometimes represented on foot, with a short garment cinched at the waist. When they were on horseback, they wore the colourful *anaxirides* (long pants of oriental origin). When leading chariots, they wore the long garments of the oracles.

Bas-relief of the Two Brothers Sarcophagus, Naples

ANCIENT ITALIC PEOPLES

The grottoes and caves of the Ligurian litoral in insular regions (Sicily and Sardinia) and some settlements built on pillars in marsh and lake regions testify to a human presence in Italy whose lifestyle was adopted by Bronze Age human beings. Archaelogists speculate these humans were of African origin, like many other western Mediterranean peoples such as, for example, the ones who built the mysterious nuraghes in Sardinia.

The humans of the Trana peat bog lived from hunting, grazing and raising animals. They also practiced farming and interacted with other groups of humans. Along with the production of stone, terracotta, wood, horn, bone and metal tools, they engaged in textile activity, as evidenced by the discovery of a spindle whorl. The Umbri, later called the Italic people, lived in central Italy.

Statue of a warrior

Capestrano warrior, Italy

ETRUSCANS

The Etruscans, originally from Asia Minor, had contact with Villanovan culture and settled in central Italy, integrating with indigenous Italic peoples established in the region at the end of the Neolithic Period.

Etruscan civilization, which emerged in the 5th century B.C., was definitivelty incorporated into Roman culture by the 1st century B.C., following a long process of cultural assimilation. There are many similarities in religion, art and clothing with Aegean region and Anatolian peoples and the Roman world, but also significant differences that evidence an autonomous and genuine evolutionary process. Etruscan women, in contrast to Greek and Roman women, occupied an important place in society and kept their surnames when they married.

Without going so far as to say it was a true matriarchy, we can assume that, given the fact that men were primarily engaged in weapons-related activities, *Etruscan* women enjoyed privileges that allowed them to be proprietors of businesses and to own slaves. When the husband died, the wife assumed the responsibility of

Tomb of the Triclinium dancers, Tarquinia

ensuring family continuity and economic assets. Nor were women prohibited from participating in symposiums and gymnastics, especially if they were from an aristocratic family.

The Etruscans preferred simple yet elegant unisex attire that highlighted the beauty of the human form. The saying "to dress a *la* Etruscan" was popular among Romans and indicated a level of refinement they did not possess.

The Etruscans cultivated art, which was closely linked to all manifestations of daily life.

The *tebenna*, with its characteristic horsehoe-shaped pattern, served as a shawl or cloak, depending on its size. It was always adorned with large, bright, contrasted trim that followed the curved or rectangular outline of the garment. Worn in a variety of ways, it is considered the most representative element of Etruscan attire. Musicians and dancers wore the tebenna, without any other garment, to cover the nude torso, with the curved part in front and the two bands falling down the back. Zither players wore it asymmetrically with one band, held in place in the pit of the arm, passing under the right arm while the other fell gracefully down the left arm. The fabrics made of wool, often very colourful, in contrast to linen, whose natural color they did not alter.

Iconographic testimony of the paintings that decorated the walls of the tombs in the Necropolis of Tarquinia suggest the likely use of gold stitching.

A typical garment worn by men was the loincloth. Not very young men and women wore long tunics, at times combined with a felt or cloth-embroidered hat. The typical cap, the *tutulus*, had a pointed tip.

Of particular interest is Etruscan footwear, which consisted of shoes or boots made with leather or embroidered cloth. Wood-sole sandals were more ergonomic thanks to a curve in the centre that allowed for bending the foot. Sandals of oriental inspiration with the tip curving upwards were very elegant.

Hairstyles and the garments of both sexes were embellished with artisanal objects of high artistic quality: diadems, earrings, bracelets, rings and brooches of bronze, silver or electrum, a commonly used gold and silver alloy.

THE ROMAN EMPIRE

Roman society adopted the cultural heritage of Greece, utilising its knowledge, procedures, daily customs and religious beliefs. From simple shepherds, the Romans evolved into a cosmopolitan people organised under an institutional and military government that proved very effective in conflicts with other major contemporary civilisations. The great expansionist ambitions of Rome dramatically extended its borders from Britannia to Spain and from Macedonia to northern Africa, including Asia Minor. The rich provincial territories were governed locally but controlled by a central power that started out as a monarchy and later became a republic, ultimately becoming a vast and powerful empire whose boundaries were identified with the limits of the civilised world. In Rome, patricians and plebeians lived alongside people of all types of subjugated ethnicities, artisans and merchants that contributed to an ever increasing prosperity.

Villa of the Mysteries, Pompey

ROMAN JEWELLERY

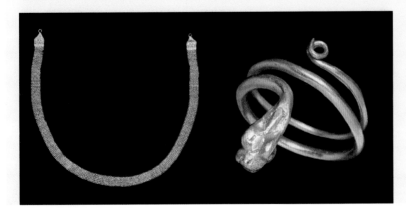

The use of jewellery was very much in vogue: metal snoods for the head, buckles, diadems, hairpins, amber bracelets, glass rings and earrings, necklaces made from glass paste and granules of gold, pendants and cameos, which highlighted the chest and face and encircled the arms and ankles. Two-and-half-metre-long necklaces traversed the entire body, first surrounding the neck, then crossing under the breasts and finally fastening on the back.

Villa Romana del Casale mosaics,
Piazza Armerina, Sicily

UNDERGARMENTS

Roman clothing distinguishes outer garments from undergarments. Undergarments, in direct contact with the skin, were different from the clothes that were worn on top and used to appear in public. Well-off people of both sexes wore the *subucula*, a thin linen or light wool shirt. Men combined it with a loincloth, the *subligaculum*. To cover the legs in harsh climates, they adopted the *tibialia* and *femoralia*, protective bands wrapped around the limbs also used by women. Women's undergarments consisted of a band worn over the breasts, the *strophium*, which later evolved into a kind of bra, the *mammillare*. The lower region was wrapped in a special garment, known as *feminalia*, for older women, while virgins used a high band of fabric that indicated their status.

Villa Borghese mosaic, Rome

ROMAN FOOTWEAR

Roman footwear appropriated the style of the Greek sandal. Men in togas wore the *calceus*, either black or red, with a flat sole and the upper part of the foot protected by a toecap or soft leather straps interwoven up to the calf. Soldiers and common men wore more practical models such as the *pero*, fastened with buckles, and the *caliga*, with a nail-studded sole, that revealed the toes. Women's footwear, finer and more elegant, was made of soft leather dyed red or gold and embellished with metal elements, cameos and precious stones.

Plato's Academy, Pompey, 1st century A.D.

Dioscorides, *Gemma Augustea*, 12th c. A.D., Vienna

The toga is the definitive representation of the ancient Roman citizen. It consisted of a broad piece of unstitched cloth, either rectangular or elliptical, that was draped around the naked body. The composition of the fabric indicated class differences: fine wool was the prerogative of patricians while plebeian togas were made of resistant materials such as hemp and yute. The Romans became experts in wool. They introduced shearing methods with curved scissors and created specifically equipped industrial facilities and workshops such as the ones discovered in Pompey, where they experimeted with batting, bleaching and dyeing methods. From wool they obtained felt, which was used with leather, to make hats, footwear, breastplates and cloaks, especially for military purposes.

Very fine linen, of higher quality than the variety that the Etruscans cultivated, came from Egypt. Cotton and silk arrived to the Port of Ostia via the provinces of Damascus and Syria. Cloths

adorned with purple bands or gold embroidery were combined with simpler, vibrantly dyed fabrics that were soft to the touch. Transparent veils, which "they wore without covering the figure", produced on the island of Cos were highly appreciated for garments. Used in ceremonies and performances, they were also used to make bedroom curtains. In the final years of the empire, entire fortunes were spent on high-in-demand exotic merchanise as the wealthy sought to obtain a degree of luxury so out of proportion that it ended up impovershing and weakening, both financially and morally as well, the pragmatic Latin people. The feminine equivalent of the toga was the stola, a long sleeveless garment worn over a tunic. The stola was made in different forms, varying the pleats of the draping, the garment's length and form and the number of brooches and adornments, always in keeping with one's role in society.

The fabrics used to make women's garments were more colourful than the ones used to produce men's clothes. They were usually woven at home, by spinning wool and linen, but dyed in specialised workshops to benefit from the expertise of dyers who had come to Rome from the eastern provinces. The *palle*, a mantle that covered the shoulders and could go over the head, was draped elegantly over the stole. Hairstyles were very important. Romans gathered their hair in complex arrangements with curls, ribbons and hairpieces. A feather fan, the *sudarium* (a handkerchief used to clean the face) and parasol served as accessories. During the wedding ritual of *confarreatio*, the bride's head was covered with the *flammeum*, a wedding veil of striking colour (red, orange or yellow) which, according to diverse literary testimonies, fell over the face to conceal the virginal flush. Even in simple form, Roman attire had an imposing structure, as befitted a conquering people.

Left: *Venus of Morgantina*, Sicily

THE TOGA

The use of the toga marked the passage from adolescence to adulthood. When a male turned seventeen, he was presented with the toga *virilis*, made of white wool, in a symbolic ceremony. During childhood, tribunes and aristocrats wore the toga *praetexta*, with a purple stripe on its border and coupled with the *bulla*, a special juvenile necklace. The type of draping, more or less ornate, gave rise to diverse models that had varying number of pleats and different names given to the curves and volumes such as *umbo*, *balteus* and *sinus*. To this end, the slaves in charge of managing the wardrobe would carefully place the cloth on wooden hangers that functioned like mannequins. The *subligaculum*, a cloth that wrapped around the body, was worn under the toga. The toga *candida* was synonymous with moral integrity and worn by men who aspired to be elected to the senate. The toga *picta* was purple, adorned with embroidery and precious stone inserts and worn by victorious generals in parades and processions. The toga

palmata, designed to exalt military valour, had purple borders and gold decorations with palm and basil-leaf motifs. The toga *sordida* was of dark and indefinite colour and was worn during funerals and tragic events.

BODY CARE

Roman women devoted a great deal of attention their physical appearance and used round, oval or square metal mirrors, as evidenced by the numerous toiletries articles found in archaeological excavations. They bleached their skin with alabaster powders and manure-based pomades while the use of Lebanon-cedar oil granted it elasticity.
Men also removed or shaved their body hair, moisturised their skin with balsam oils, wore makeup and, hedonists that they were, used perfumes with essences extracted from garden plants which they kept in beautiful opaline-glass bottles. For theatre perfomances, the velarium, a large cloth that protected the spectators in the ampitheatre from the sun, was sprayed with perfumed water.

Men and women frequented thermal establishments, one of the preferred pastimes of rich patricians, to revitalise the body and spirit. They strolled among fountains adorned with nymphs and conversed pleasantly on the edge of the hot pool and the *tepi-darium*, surrrounded by attentive slaves and servants.
To be more attractive, matrons dyed their hair, and their hairstyles, which were initially simple, became more and more elaborate during the imperial age. They also combed their hair in braids and used hair-pieces to reinforce the structure of the oblong gathered sections interlaced with ribbons and little silk strings, so intricate that they appeared to be wigs.

Diana and Spring, fresco, Stabia (Naples)

Right: Roman helmet

Below: Vibia Sabina marble (Rome)

FIRST CENTURIES OF THE CHRISTIAN ERA

In the first centuries of the Christian era, more and more of the faithful gathered in the catacombs to pray and hear the word of God, who professed unconditional love for all human beings. A desire for simplicity and new values gradually triumphed, resulting in more restrained tastes regarding one's physical appearance and manner of dress.

Instead of the luxurious draping effects of the stola and toga, which were no longer obligatory on special occasions, austere, rudimentary tunics, cut and sewn in oriental fashion, were preferred. They consisted of a single piece of fabric, folded lengthwise with a simple opening for the head, sewn at the sides and attached to the waist by a belt. As a result of the new moral codes, it seemed necessary to introduce the use of long, narrow sleeves that covered the arms completely. The tunic was more closefitting and was widely accepted. These linen garments, which were worn in direct contact with the skin, are the origin of the shirt.

The new manner of dressing that developed from the 3rd to the 4th century A.D. is documented in paintings and mosaics from the Roman period. The Christian Copts wore these same tunics, which were made of natural linen or were white with polychromatic decorations, though woven or embroidered with wool, vertical, parallel or symmetrical bands called clavias, which went up the back and chest and ended in a sharp point. The preference for animal fibres had symbolic value; it was associated with the sacrificial lamb, an important image in Christian mystical iconography.

Both men and women continued to wear cloaks, though women preferred the shawl, which prevented them from making an overly ostentatious exhibition of their beauty and called attention to the virtues of chastity, humility and submissiveness, characteristics of women's designs for many centuries to come.

5th century tunic

Amazon sarcophagus, Tarquinia

BYZANTINES

The mosaics in the Basilica of Sant'Apollinare Nuovo and the Basilica of San Vitale (5th and 6th centuries) restored ostentation and opulence, symbols of political and religious power in Byzanntine culture. In the ceremony of consecration, the emperor Justinian (527-565) and his wife Theodora, surrounded by dignitaries and ladies, appeared in a hieratic and solemn pose, completely enveloped in the heavy drapery of their garments, the form of which recalled the heavy fabrics of the Roman nobility, though more austere and reflective of Middle Eastern influences.

The basic garment was the white tunic, long for women and short for men, with close-fitting sleeves adorned with circles, bars and patagium (gold-embroidered band) over which a very ornate silk dalmatica was worn. The use of jewellery highlighted the elegance of the figures. The empress' wide cloak is a dark purple chlamys with a genuine masterpiece embroidered in the background representing the Adoration of the Magi. The inner tunic was also embellished with high quality borders in gold. Theodora wore a diadem adorned with *pendilia*, long dangling ornaments consisting of pearls, and a gorgeous gem necklace, the *maniakion*, which surrounded the shoulders. Justinian, in addition to a crown with side pendants, wore an eye-catching broach with pearls that fastened his cloak, decorated on both sides with a *tablion*, a rectangular panel of embroidered cloth.

Men had beards and short hair. Women used ribbons or bejewelled snood bonnets to hold their hair in place. All the suits of the Byzanntine court embodied diverse decorative techniques: multicoloured brocades, bright thread inserts, needle embroidery and gem applications. Silk threads, perfumes, spices and precious stones of all kinds arrived to Byzantium, situated on the banks

Justinian and his court, San Vital mosaic, Ravena, mid 6th century

Empress Theodora, San Vitale, Ravena, mid 6th century

of the Bosphorous River, from Asia, and commercial interchange contributed to increasing the country's wealth. Purple became exclusive to the basileus, or emperor, and the imperial family, according to precise standards of etiquette that assigned the use of colour and decorations based on rank. The emperor Justinian, also the highest ranking official of the Church, adopted it in memory of the red robe of Christ. The colour purple, in all of its tones, was obtained through various dyeing cycles: ruby, bright red, carmine, hyacinth and dark violet. Hues of blue, green and apricot pink, always associated with gold, were also used. The rearing of silk-worms, implemented in 552 under an imperial monopoly, allowed for the production of brightly coloured *samite* (a heavy silk fabric made up of six threads) interwoven with gold threads and animal representations contained in Iranian-style tangent circles.

The importance of silk hanging ornaments in palace and church decorations is undeniably apparent in the Basilica of Saint Sophia, in Constantinople, where tapestries that tell stories for liturgical purposes hang from columns. Cloths and garments, woven with precious metals, represent important courtesy attendants directed at foreign sovereigns. Footwear similar to slippers could be made of soft silk and decorated with Persian-style embroidery. Colours varied: black for dignitaries and red or yellow with gold buckles and precious stones for sovereigns.

Combining Greco-Roman cultural inheritance with Christian and oriental symbols, artisans specialised in high-quality ornamental techniques, achieving an impressive level of refinement that would become a distinctive feature of Byzantine aesthetics. Their work, supported and valued by a politico-religious hierarchichal system, would have a tremendous influence on artistic fields in the coming centuries.

Peoples of antiquity   39

Middle Ages

THE MIGRATION PERIOD AND THE BARBARIAN INVASIONS

Shiite cup, 4th century

Within the confines of the vast imperial possessions, the migratory flow of different nomadic tribes of Germanic and Asian origin gave way to invasions of "rough and primitive" peoples, heretofore unknown. The Huns, warriors of Siberian origin, made incursions against the western Roman Empire at the end of the 5th century. About them the historian Ammianus (XXXI, 2) wrote: "They wore garments made of linen or woodchuck skins, and they used one type of attire at home and another outside. But once they put on a faded tunic, they would not discard or change it until, damaged because of extensive wear, it was reduced to rags". Vandals, Visigoths, Suebi, Burgundians, Franks, Bretons, Anglo-Saxons and Celts settled in Western Europe. The variety of origins, climates and degree of cultural development of these peoples meant different attire, but the essentially primitive character of them all limited the elements of their clothing to tunics made of coarse fabric and short coats made of fur that tied to the waist with a strap. When riding horseback, they wrapped their thighs with short, tight trousers made of goat skin or fabric tied to the legs with intersecting cords. The cloak was fastened to the chest or around the neck with one or more fibulae or brooches. On their feet, they wore leather shoes adapted to the latitudes they inhabited: open shoes or sandals for warmer areas, leather calf-high or above-the-knee boots, lined with leather, for colder regions. Long capes over the shoulders and unkempt beards increased the menacing appearance of the men, reinforced by felted wool caps and helmets with protuberant horns. Women also wore cloaks of different widths made of coarse wool dyed in bright colors, in addition to long skirts attached to the waist with carved needles or metal belts. Women never cut their hair, parting it in two long side braids.

In 486, Theodoric, king of the Ostrogoths, who had been raised in the refinement of Constantinople, occupied Italy. Successive waves of other peoples attracted by Rome's wealth invaded the Italian peninsula.

Viking helmet and sword

EARLY MEDIEVAL ATTIRE, ANCIENT EUROPEAN PEOPLES

In the early Middle Ages (6th to 10th centuries), society was hierarchically organized. Clothes were expensive, and what somebody wore identified and differentiated social groups depending on their economic status, maintaining and reinforcing their collective identity. Power and wealth were exhibited in garments made of brightly coloured silk, adornments fashioned from gemstones and metal ornaments that powerfully stood out against the modest, faded materials of peasants' clothes. The most commonly used fibre throughout the region was felted, combed and ultimately dyed wool. Linen was used to make light garments and undergarments, the production of which for a long time was a domestic chore.

Silk, always reserved for a select elite, was to a large extent supplied by distant oriental markets. The basic garment of the early medieval wardrobe was the long-sleeve tunic, which covered the body without any suggestion of the shapes underneath. It was long and straight for women while shorter and with a cut similar to a nightgown for men, which they wore on top of trousers. Other superimposed tunics, decorated with large trimmings in bright colors, were cinched with a belt and created various combinations that allowed for differentiating class and caste, as well as free men from slaves. Types of tunics and their accessories also facilitated identifying the different professions and recognising vassals, vassals of vassals, soldiers and knights, priests and religious men of numerous orders, citizens, passers-by, outsiders, etc. For protection from the elements, they wore cloaks of varying widths and shapes made of heavy wool with visible weaves or ones made of leather which fastened to the shoulders with needles and brooches.

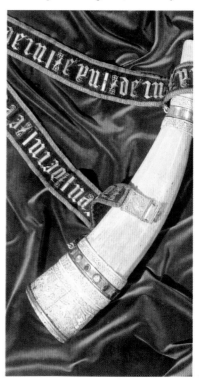

Charlemagne's hunting horn, 9th century

LOMBARDS

The Lombards, who dominated Italy between 568 and 774, were known for their skills as woodworkers and metal smiths as well as for creating paneling in wood and bronze. They worked with gold and silver employing the *niello* technique (incisions in the metal inlaid with a black mixture) and decorated these objects with mounts of precious and semiprecious stones in the shape of a teardrop or a heart. After embracing Christianity in the 7th century, they adopted golden crosses and the two-headed eagle, and women ceased piercing their ears to wear earrings, a custom considered by the church as barbarian, characteristic of infidels and Saracens.

When the barbarian peoples came into contact with the refined ex-subjects of the Roman Empire and the courts of the ancient European peoples – Carolingians, Saxons and Normans – , the need to definitively seal the power of the military and the church emerged. Clothes were embellished, and more close-fitting long-sleeved tunics, made of linen or fine wool, were adopted. On top of them, other bell-shaped garments were worn, which were made of wool or silk in multiple colors and had embroidered hems and shorter sleeves. The attire was completed with a cape that reached the ankles. The footwear of the nobility and kings and queens was adorned with metal and stone inlays.

Lombard king with his vassals

Merovingian fibula

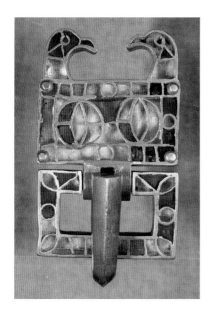

CAROLINGIANS

In the 11th century, the Francs assumed the central role in European history. In response to the call of the popes, and guided by King Charles – called Charlemagne because of his great deeds as a defender of Christianity – the Francs unified the different territories that constituted the Holy Roman Empire (France, Belgium, Holland, Germany, Switzerland, Austria and Northern and Central Italy). To rule these lands, Charlemagne, crowned emperor in 80 AD, instituted the feudal system of division of properties according to a rigid pyramidal system of distribution among vassals, vassals of vassals and citizens, who divided economic and political power among themselves. The clothes worn by Charlemagne, who remained loyal to Frankish uses and customs, was quite simple, while court subjects lived immersed in exaggerated luxury, contrary to the stipulations of a set of sumptuary laws that regulated even the specific use of fabric. According to his biographer Einhard, Charlemagne wore linen shirts and trousers, a tight fitting tunic tied with a silk belt, an otter-skin vest and leather leggings. On top of these garments he wore the *sago veneto*, a Gallic-style cloak, and a gold and silver sword. Only for official occasions did Charlemagne abandon his soldier attire and don a suit woven in gold, precious shoes with gemstones and a cloak and diadem, all in keeping with his status. A dalmatic embroidered with religious scenes narrating the Transfiguration of Christ and the Last Judgement, preserved in the Vatican's Saint Peter's Treasury,

Carolingian earring

Charlemagne, Aachen cathedral, Germany

may have been the one that the monarch had on for his coronation. Carolingians favoured strong colours combined in contrasting tones. They wore their hair short and square, and grew thick and long moustaches. During the Merovingian period, in France, people wore the *gonelle*, a linen tunic that reached the calves with gold embroideries and that fastened with a belt. Women wore two tunics of different lengths. Part of the garment underneath was therefore visible, with wide and extremely long sleeves and with precious embroideries on the neckline, cuffs and hem. They wore their hair in long bejeweled tresses and covered their heads with a veil that differentiated married women from maidens, the latter ones showing their hair.

Left: Iron crown

Frankish helmet

SAXONS

Between the 10th and 11th centuries, the Ottonian or Saxon dynasty reigned in Germany, Switzerland, Burgundy and northern Italy, helping to secure the power of the bishops in the political and economic sphere. The Saxons were responsible for an economic resurgence that entailed solid commercial development, strengthened thanks to the traffic of the first maritime republics. A miniature dating from the end of the 10th century and preserved in Monaco shows four female figures, representing the four imperial regions (Slavic countries, Germania, Gaul, and Rome) and honouring Otto III, dressed in tunics and bright coloured cloaks. Initially, clerical attire was nearly indistinguishable from its secular counterpart, though over time it adopted recognisable liturgical features, consisting of the dalmatic, chasuble and cloak. While bishops and prelates used precious fabrics such as bright silk from Constantinople, monks

Otto III honoured by the four regions of the empire

and pilgrims wore a coarse smock with a hood. Clerical garments were the first to incorporate embroidered ornaments as a symbol of the power and prestige that their wearers wanted to exhibit. The chasubles of Saints Herlindis and Relindis of Maaseik (850 AD), made in England, are the oldest manufactured garments produced in Europe. Another example of an Anglo-Saxon garment is the stole and maniple of Saint Cuthbert (909-916 AD) ordered by Aelflaed, wife of Edward the Old, for Frithestan, Bishop of Winchester.

Bayeux Tapestry, detail (France)

NORMANS

The northern peoples – Scandinavians, Anglo-Saxons and Normans – that inhabited the coast were great seafarers as well as warriors. When they occupied the northeastern region of France (845 A.D-911 A.D.), which was christened Normandy, they came into contact, albeit indirectly, with Roman civilization, from which they appropriated customs and traditions. The Bayeux Tapestry (Bayeux, Bayeux Museum), a large "textile fresco" consisting of a wool embroidery over a linen background, contains sequences of logistic preparations, war scenes and daily life that illustrate aspects

Bayeux Tapestry, detail (France)

and details of men's attire in the time of William the Conqueror, Duke of Normandy, during the Battle of Hastings, which led to his conquest of England, then known as Britannia. The tapestry was exhibited in Bayeux Cathedral to spread a political message among the faithful and to legitimise the right to the English throne. Among scholars of military history, this piece is considered an essential documentary source of the weapons and armour used in the second half of the 11th century. The Norman knight's equipment consisted of a light coat of mail without lining made with thousands of woven iron rings to create a flexible tunic, along with trousers of the same material. Called the *haubert* or *brogne*, it was worn for military operations. The sleeves were wide to provide freedom of movement to the arms. This combat attire substituted the leather tunic covered with metallic scales that was used until the 11th century. The head was protected with a hood also made of mail, on top of which the warrior wore a helmet with a protective piece for the nose. The almond-shaped shield, which was made of wood and covered with leather, bore heraldry emblems in its centre. The horses were adorned with chest guards refined harnesses, chest guards, stomach guards and a comfortable saddle.

FEUDAL SOCIETY, MONASTIC LIFE AND MILITARY ORDER. THE CRUSADES

Life in medieval society revolved around prayer, arduous toiling of the soil and the practice of arms in defense of the fief. Peasants represented the majority of the population and dedicated the bulk of their energies to survival, while monks and knights played central roles in shaping European history. The fortified castle with defensive towers and walls constituted an independent and self-sufficient unit as far as the production of basic necessities, including articles of clothing, was concerned. Men's lives were engrossed by war, undertakings full of fascination and danger. They negotiated to establish alliances or forge diplomatic agreements of solidarity or subordination. Squires and knights engaged in combat. During periods of peace, they participated in tournaments where they flaunted the necklaces and emblems of their houses and claimed the attention of the ladies or they took part in hunts with falcons, which they held on a special lined glove. Musical instruments accompanied dance performances. Charms and bells were sewn to hems of dresses and to the ends of long strips of multicoloured fabric tied to the cuffs, which were waved during traditional dances. Stories, legends and poetry written by court troubadours warmed rooms with cold stone walls hung with tapestries and heavy curtains covering the windows. During the military campaigns organised by crusaders, the knights fought under the sign of the cross against Muslim infidels in the name of the supremacy of Christianity.

Two medieval warriors with helmets and coats of mail, 12th century

Knight and lady in medieval attire, 14th century

MONASTIC LIFE

During the period of the barbarian invasions, monastic life assumed greater significance. Its nucleus was the meditative and laborious existence of the small communities of monks and hermits. Monasteries and abbeys became important cultural centres with a cloister, laboratory and library that safeguarded ancient knowledge and wisdom and promoted a religious, economic and civilian resurgence. Monks wore a tunic made of coarse, heavy wool tied to the waist with a cord. On top, they wore a long cloak with a hood. A simple wooden cross on the neck and a rosary on the waist rounded out the attire. The tone of the faded colours chosen for these simple clothes, which had to express lack and renunciation of fleshly delights, differentiated the members of the various orders. Monks wore leather sandals and carried sacks

Monk drinking, 13th century

Andrea de Bonaiuto, *Mission and triumph of the Church*, 14th century, Florence

made of the same material for alms. In the land surrounding the monasteries, they grew aromatic herbs and plants with dyeing properties, which they dried and used to make vegetable dyes for fabrics. Colours were applied by submerging the fabric in the dye that had been dissolved in boiling water, adding such fixatives as alum or salt, which acted as a mordant to ensure that the colour would hold fast and not fade. The monks transmitted this practice and zealously guarded the recipes for the dyes. They also specialised in the production of woolen fabrics, which required a long production process and several stages of preparation: from sifting to washing to combing to carding, spinning, weaving, beating, trimming, brushing and, finally, dyeing. Later, business owners and merchants produced woolen fabrics, commissioning the work to shops and specialised workers.

Philosophy lessons in Paris, end of 14th century

LIFE OF MEDIEVAL KNIGHTS

During the tournaments of the 12th century, emblems of the noble houses were exhibited on standards, horse blankets and flags. Once a knight put on the coat of mail, armour and other equipment that protected most of his body, he became unrecognizable. The cylin-

Knightly life, 14th century

drical helmet had a cross-shaped opening in front, or, alternatively, it was round and had a wavy feather. Shields and helmets had simple symbols with bright and contrasting colours – red, yellow, blue and white, black and green – that could be recognized from a distance. The colours had symbolic meaning: red for bravery, white for honour, blue for pride and green for fertility. Yellow and grey represented gold and silver.

The upper garment, both for men and women, was the *bliaud*. It had long sleeves hanging open from the elbow, revealing the sleeves of the chainse (a white tunic made of cloth that served as a shirt), cinched and fastened thanks to a row of small buttons. Pageboys, heralds, squires, archers and armour bearers wore dress coats and tabards emblazoned with emblems.

THE CRUSADES

The Crusades ignited the religious spirit and knightly desire to liberate the Holy Sepulchre. Between the 11th and 13th centuries, in the region of Anatolia and the eastern Mediterranean, as well as in Egypt and Tunisia, the troops of the Christian countries of Europe fought the Muslim armies. The aristocratic warrior class influenced attire in every respect. The term *cruzado* is a Spanish word that identifies the "wearer of the cross". Indeed, the soldiers of Christ wore on their chest a piece of white fabric with a red cross, an emblem that appeared on their standards as well. Even though the Crusades took many Christian lives, they also had fruitful economic results. Among the outstanding Italian cities were the maritime republics of Pisa, Genoa, Venice and Amalfi, whose

TAILORING

Tailors, Issogne

With the disappearance of Roman attire, the first cut and sewn garments appeared, thereby increasing the prestige of the tailoring trade, consolidated in middle of the 12th century. During medieval times it was considered a *light* trade, because to open a tailor shop, only a few simple tools were needed: scissors of varying size, needles and thimbles made of bone or bronze, thread, sticks and strings to take measurements and wax tablets to take notes. However, to be a tailor required great skill and precision, as well as profound technical knowledge passed on from father to son. A school for tailors existed as early as 1102.

A professional hierarchy governed the exercise of the art of tailoring: the tailor cut the garment while assistants and apprentices sewed and refined it. In the workshop, other tailoring-related activities might occur, such as embroidering and the manufacture of accessories and fur and leather articles. This is the reason why there was such a close relationship between tailors and the manufacturers of luxury goods. The trade used to be the prerogative of men, the *masters*, who used female labour specializing in sewing. Caravans from foreign lands spread new fashions that used fabrics, colours and materials that were otherwise rare and difficult to find in isolated local medieval cultures.

powerful fleets transported exotic embroidered fabrics, furs, spices and precious stones. The growth of the merchant class favoured the circulation and expansion of knowledge and the revival of the arts in general.

Crusaders, 13th century

Knights in the conquest of Antioquia, 14th century

Ascent to calvary, 14th century

FAR AND NEAR
EAST CHINA

Attire in distant China varied depending on social class and geography. Sericulture, or silk farming, had been known since the third millennium B.C., and peasants secretly engaged in this activity at home. Textile workshops produced elaborate muslin, satin and velvet in bright colours that were subject to strict control by the state, which supervised and managed all aspects of production through its representatives. Silk fabrics could be found in the wardrobe of the nobility, whose members wore light, long cloaks with long sleeves and many superimposed layers. Peasants wore clothes made of hemp and bamboo fibre, conical-shaped hats and shoes made of braided straw. Precious fabrics were used as well to pay taxes or reward local administrators. They were also given as gifts to ambassadors of foreign countries, served as bargaining chips to acquire horses and other goods and were given as presents to ensure peace in political negotiations. All Chinese decorative motifs have symbolic value. The design of new trends and reproductions of cups or effigies of mythological animals such as the dragon or phoenix were reserved for the emperor's clothes and those of his consort. Polychromatic silk embroidery, an art in which the Chinese were unparalleled masters, was of great importance. The Chinese invented a repertoire of stitches which they alternated with silk painting. Frequently, they also depicted ideograms. Women wore long, open, crossover tunics over a skirt (in the north) or wide trousers (in the south) tied with a belt made of a series of hanging straps. Since they did not have pockets, the dresses came with fabric pouches that hung from the waist and were used to hold fans, flasks of perfume,

Servant and male terracotta figures from the northern Wei dynasty (386-581), China

purses and other personal items. The colours and emblems were connected to life cycles in the natural world. Primary colours were reserved for the nobility, while commoners used complementary colours. For ceremonies, the Chinese wore overcoats with bell-shaped sleeves that were so long they dragged them on the floor or delicately folded them along the arms. During the Tang dynasty, women wore three-piece dresses consisting of a short shirt, a tight, long skirt and a bodice with a three-quarter sleeve. The Chinese wore silk slippers with curved points and high hats on top of their long hair, gathered in a bun. The terracotta warriors discovered in the tomb of Qin Shi Huang are dressed in military attire consisting of a short bell-shaped piece and wide trousers on top of which they are wearing armour. The armour consists of a jacket with rectangular plates tied to the sides, closed around the neck with a scarf and with a short cape around the shoulders.

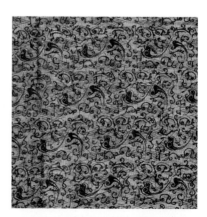

Chinese tunic

Right: painting on canvass, China, 9th century

Noble women going on a horseback ride,
copy by Li Kong Ling, 12th century

Chinese women making silk

JAPAN

The Japanese national garment is the kimono, identical for both men and women. The only difference is that women used the obi, a wide sash made of fabric of up to 5 metres long placed between the waist and the buttocks and tied at the back with an elaborate knot shaped like a cushion. The kimono is T-shaped, rather bulky and comes in different versions: with narrow sleeves *(kosode)*, wide sleeves *(hirosode)* or hanging sleeves *(furisode)*. The accessories hanging from the waist, called inro, were boxes containing personal seals and wax. Later, they became little purses to carry charms and small sewing kits.

Japanese fabrics have elegant intertwined motifs and include decorations with various colour effects obtained with materials and by employing the *shibori* technique. Silk fabric was also used to create the *kesa*, a rectangle of woven silk obtained with tapestry technique, creating a kind of mandala symbolizing the four points of the compass, that is linked to the rituals in Buddhist temples.

Beauty and fertility, miniature and silk book

INDIA

The primitive peoples that occupied the Indian subcontinent and the Indus Basin since antiquity (4000 B.C.) grew linen, a fibre particularly suitable for the local climate, which they used to weave the subtle veils that they wore. The colours were bright and luminous, the product of their mastery of dyeing techniques, and enriched with precious stones. Throughout the ages, peoples of different natures and religions formed a mixture of races that converged in India, resulting in a great variety of clothing. The most widely held beliefs were Hinduism and Buddhism, while in the Middle Ages some people began to embrace the Islamic faith. Society was strictly divided into classes: priests, nobility and warriors, merchants, peasants and, at the bottom, serfs. Cotton was widely known. Used locally for everyday attire, it was exported to the West, where it was used to line military cuirasses. The Indians produced a type of silk, obtained from wild silkworms collected

Murals with deities

56

Miniature

Silk book

in the woods, that was coarser and more irregular than the silk that farmed Chinese and Persian silkworms produced. Hindus considered silk a pure material and, thus, adequate for religious purposes. Articles of clothing ranged from plain cotton dresses for common people to more affected apparel, in purple and brocade, for princes. Cut and sewn dresses such as the *angarkha*, which was open and reached down to the calf, the *jama*, a ceremonial tunic, and the *chuga* cloak, were worn by the upper classes and considered distinguished in comparison to unsewn dresses, such as the *dhoti* (a loincloth) or the *lungi* (a short skirt) that wrapped around the buttocks and were typically worn by commoners. The *sari*, a term derived from the Sanskrit *chaira*, which means "piece of fabric for dressing", appeared around the 2nd century and has endured as a typically feminine garment for thousands of years. Many women wore saris, still considered today a symbol of India and the strong link between women and tradition. The sari, made of a fabric spun on a loom, is between 5 and 7 metres long with ornamented hems. It envelops the body and can be draped in a thousand graceful ways.

The sari, which was worn on top of a bodice with narrow sleeves, can function as a dress, shawl, cloak or veil. The head was covered with bonnets, turbans, tiaras and conical hats. The medieval age was the period of greatest development of Hindu culture.

TURKEY

The Tartars, who in remote times had reached the Mediterranean basin in present-day Turkey, inhabited northern China. They were a fierce people that dressed in furs. Tartar women wrapped themselves in heavy, wide dresses that remained unchanged in the Far East and Siberia, rarely incorporating Chinese fashions. Instead, Chinese style prospered in Turkey: women adopted silk brocade tunics with long, wide sleeves and wore overcoats and cloaks on top. They covered their faces with a veil, as dictated by the rules of the prophet Mohammed. At home, the attire was freer and included a small sleeveless bolero-type corset, which left the belly exposed, with wide trousers that tied at the ankles. The arms were adorned with splendid jewellery, and on their feet, fitted with small chains, they wore slippers with an arched toe. The bolero is a Hindu piece of clothing that the Arabs disseminated throughout Spain and the Mediterranean.

ARAB PEOPLES

Organised into mutually hostile tribes, the Arabs lived in the oasis and inhospitable areas of the Arab peninsula. The Bedouins had a nomadic life in the desert and rode their camels trading products along caravan routes. They expanded their territory eastward and became acquainted with China, Central Asia and India. They spread the technique of compound weaving throughout the West. Islamic fabrics (from "islam", which means "submission to God") were religious in nature and contained calligraphic inscriptions distributed in horizontal bands, which praised God and the caliph, the head of the community. These inscriptions, made in letters of the Kufic alphabet, from Kufa, a flourishing cultural centre in times of the Umayyad dynasty, were either woven or embroidered. They were made of linen, cotton, wool and silk, in addition to camel and goat hair for felts, palm fibres, linen and woven hair. By the 8th

Battle scene of the *Poem of Alexander*, Turkish miniature, 15th century and Persian

century, fabrics were already being produced made in state-owned workshops called *tiraz*, which monopolized the industry and the sector's commerce to benefit princes and caliphs. Arabs wore a long shirt that reached the calves, with long sleeves extending to the tips of the fingers, that was often open at the chest and a red scarf tied around the waist. Some miniatures document the use of brightly coloured kaftans and gold ornaments even in stores and camel blankets, as well as complicated turbans that men wore wrapped around their heads. Latin peoples imitated the Arab hood together with the short cape. Confined to the harem, women wore wide trousers under long tunics and covered their heads with veils. The first capital of the Islamic empire was Damascus, a city named after a type of monochromatic compound fabric with bright and opaque effects. The Arab tradition benefited from technical and cosmopolitan cultural contributions inherited from conquered and, later, assimilated peoples. The Arabs attributed a great deal of importance to the principles of harmony, geometry and compositional balance, which had a profound effect on the arts. In addition to the contri- bution of calligraphy, fabric decorations were enriched with other stylised elements such as arabesques and braids, which appeared in architecture and in many decorations of sculpted and painted wood.

Muslim silk fabric, 11th century

Al-Hariri's maqama, *Listening to the Theologian*, 1237

CLOTHING IN URBAN COMMUNITIES

The 12th century was a period of transition and renewal. Feudalism was entering a state of crisis and many people whose survival depended on the harsh realities of working in the fields moved to the small urban centres that had begun to take shape, forming armies and administrative organisations. In Italy, the political expression of these socio-economic changes could been seen in urban townships in which universities and artisanal activities began to flourish. Professions associated with clothing became specialised, benefitted from innovations, acquired increased economic importance and were organised under art and trade cooperatives, entities which not only supervised and protected professional activities but also exercised a degree of political influence and participated in government. In addition, they established rules

Shirt production, *Tacuinum Sanitatis*

regarding work quality: hierarchies, allocation of tasks, standards for apprenticeships (which lasted many years), wages and types of products that weavers, tapestry makers, dyers, tailors, cutters, silk and gold embroiderers, shoemakers of different kinds, decorators furriers, gunsmiths and decorators, to name a few, were authorised to produce and punch mark with their stamp.

To avoid competition, sales prices were set according to the characteristics of the goods. Fabrics and clothing were sold at trade fairs held in Flanders, a region renamed for the production of wool and linen. Important markets that specialised in international transactions of luxury goods could be found In SainT-Denis, the Champagne region and Pavia. The city, a privileged place for the creation and production of fashion, also became the setting for exhibiting the newest clothing, as social status depended more on wealth than lineage. Throughout western Europe, the human body adopted the stylised features that can be observed in the postures of sculptures.

Mangravio Ekkenhard and his wife,
13th century, Naumburgo, Germany

Women wore loose-fitting tunics cinched at the bust that highlighted curves and fell to the feet while, in the back, the garment continued in the form of a tail. Needless to say, the Church was quick to express its disapproval. In the chronicle *Ecclesiasticae Historiae XIII*, Ordericus Vitalis comments on the new uses and customs, observing that "the tails of women's dresses are long, useless and serve only to collect dust." The sleeves were tightfitting up to the elbow and flared towards the cuffs. Their width came to be so exagerrated that it was necessary to knot the sleeves to avoid dragging them on the ground and tripping over them. Extremely wide sleeves was a manifestation of international fashion that can be seen in the right tynpanum of the Royal Portal Chartres in the images of the Annunciation and the Visitation. Shoes, called poulaine, had long, pointy toes with a filling that granted them rigidity, following the fashion of filing down the extremities as if they were "serpents' tails", an animal associated with the evil one. Court culture, which emerged in 12th century France, cultivated the notion of knightly virtue and the art of elegance. Knights dressed in short tunics over which they wore the *scapular* open on the sides and the family emblem embroidered on the chest. Scenes of daily life depicted in miniatures illustrate interesting details regarding people's wardrobe and hairstyles. The *gonella*, used by both sexes, had long sleeves, was tight in the waist and loose on the sides. Coats were of varying lengths and contrasting colours. Women's headwear consisted of white linen or silk bands that brushed against the cheeks and framed the face, clinging to the throat and falling freely on the shoulders. During this period, women played a prominent role, idealised in the verses of troubadours, and participated in economic development by contributing their handiwork to family workshops. Indeed, leather production and spinning and twisting of wool fabrics, as well as silk winding, were tasks performed by a female workforce, which was cheaper than its male counterpart. In the 12th century, in Italy, precious silk fabrics began to be manufactured, employing a techique that had been introduced in the Arabic workrooms established in Sicily.

Anonymous, homicide scene, 14th century

Master Gian Barrile, *Betrothal of the virgin* (detail), Naples

Garments worn by Roger II duting his coronation, Palermo, 12th century

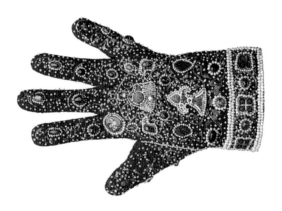

SEIGNORIES (13th-14th CENTURY)

In the 14th century, while the international Gothic style took root in northern Europe, in many Italian regions seignories, an oligarchical form of government headed by the figure of the seignor, who was responsible for guaranteeing prosperity, was established. Internecine struggles, skirmishes and rivalries that marked the triumph of local powers with the blessing and protection of the Church were rocking Italian politics. Local governments looked favourably upon investments in the textile industry and the expansion of trade across Europe, with an accumulation of resources that eventually gave rise, through bank credits, to the first commercial transactions. Economic improvement brought new dimensions of elegance and wealth to fashion. While a preference existed for the use of oriental damasks and lampas, important manufacturing sectors, organised by scores of expert artisans, were founded in Lucca, Venice, Florence and Milan. Initially, textile production mimicked exotic gold and silk designs with animal drawings requested, above all, by the clergy and sovereigns. Soon, however, the most sought after and precious fabrics were equalled and exceeded by the imaginatioin and expertise of local artisans and businessmen, who innovated compositional designs through the introduction of Gothic-style floral and plant-shoot elements.

The high incomes of the rich favoured the overall evolution of art and culture through patronage, widely dispersed across the major Italian courts. Around 1340, men's clothing began to distinguish itself from women's styles, in conformity with the Italian trend of shortening attire to the knee. The leather shirt was maintained and became an undergarment, though its length was reduced so that it could be tucked into the breeches, which were custom made and reinforced with a sole. Garments of European influence such as the

Sir Geoffry Luttrel with his wife and daughter-in-law 1335-1340, British Museum, London

doublet, introduced in France, which revealed men's well-toned legs and thighs, replaced the tunic and outer tunic. The doublet was a kind of lined vest, buttoned in the front and buckled at the waist with a ring from which a small leather pouch, called a *scarsella*, dangled "German-style". The *gonella* adopted the *ropilla*, a garment made of generally light fabrics that was cinched below the waist and flared outward from there, barely reaching below the sides. The colour of clothes had an important social function: the more eye-catching the colour, the wealthier the wearer of the garment was considered given the high price of the substances used for dyeing fabrics, which could also be of animal origin: murex for intense red and violet tones, rubia and kermes for reds, isatide for blue, migninette and saffron for yellow and leaves and bark for brown tones. Dresses and footwear were often two-toned and bore heraldic emblems and colours with stripes and lotus flowers. Over this, different types of long-sleeve overcoats were worn, in addition to wide, bell-shaped, ankle-length coats with wraparound collars that fell to the chest, similar to cloaks. Made from opulent and costly fabrics, often with leather lining, they were called the paletoque, huca, houppeland, gaban or hopa.

Influential citizens who held institutional positions continued to wear the ankle-length tunics that had emerged in the 13th century. In addition they wore cap-like hats with a raised brim, multi-coloured caps and peaked hoods such as the ones worn by the poet Dante Aligheri. The use of new hats required short hair

Portrait of Dante Alighieri

Woman's hairnet, 14th century

Simone Martini, *The Musicians*, Basilica of Asís, 1322-1326

Giotto, *The Gift of the Mantle*, Asis, 1295

for men, while the custom of curling one's hair with hot irons began to spread. During the period of the seignories, women's fashion did not undergo very many changes, while the ensemble of dressing garmets began to be referred to as "clothes". In the 14th and beginning of the 15th century, women's subordinate position persisted. Still, while women were subject to the will and authority of their husbands and their fathers, there are many examples of women who distinguished themselves on account of their courage and initiative. At the time of marriage, a father paid a dowry as compensation for the maintenance of his daughter during her future conjugal life. The dowry consisted of a sum of money, land, possessions, clothing and jewellery, as well as a coffer of personal white clothing and household items woven and sewn by the wife herself, which consisted of towels, sheets and other cloths embroidered and decorated with festoons and intricate lace. Women's fashion maintained a loose elongated structure. Daily attire consisted of three layers of clothing: the camisole, petticoat and cotehardie, which was the dress itself. Dresses were cut straight and clung slightly to the waist; skirts were floor length, densely pleated and cinched with an opulent belt. They had lengthwise openings

Ambrogio Lorenzetti, *Effects of Good Government*, Siena, 1338-1340

Andrea di Bonaiuto, *Spanish Chapel*, Florence, 1365

Allegretto Nuzi, *Voyage of Saint Ursula*, around 1365, Fabriano, Italy

at the sides, as can be seen in the young women dancing in the painting *The Effects of Good Government* by Ambrogio Lorenzetti. A deep neckline revealed the neck; it was oval, square or conical shaped so that the undergarments would be visible, with a V-cut from the shoulders to the stomach and covered with an insert to avoid incurring the disapproval of the Church.

The sleeves of undergarments, made of light but richly adorned materials, protruded from the tightfitting, funnel-shaped or very short sleeves of dresses. In the absence of valets to support the train of dresses, the custom of lifting the train up and inserting it in the bejewelled belt, revealing the lining of contrasting colours, gained popularity. Overcoats with wide sleeves, finished with openwork festoons and Gothic-style lace trim, evidenced a taste for excessive and exaggerated ornamentation. Functional and operational buttons, inserted in eyelets or clasps and with a dual

use, were made of filigreed gold or precious enamelled metals, as were buckles, fasteners and little bells. Necklaces of amber or coral were worn, in addition to numerous rings on the fingers. Hair, divided by a part in the middle, was wavy and gathered in long braids or playful *arrangements* in the form of a crown, with side bands that were held in place in a *crespina*, a hairnet formed by wire cylinders joined to a strip of cloth, or were closed with beautiful pins interspersed with crowns and diadems. The most typical examples of headdress were the chaperon, also represented by Paolo Uccello, which consisted of a filled cylinder that concealed the hair and ears and was ornamented with gold and jewels, strands of ribbons and pearls, and the cerquillos, a kind of metal ribbon, in addition to diverse silk hair coverings and gold-thread hairnets adorned with pearls and precious stones.

While married women always covered their hair, young people of both sexes wore their hair loose and adorned with wreaths. Extragavant hair styles in the form of a heart, saddle, pillow or horn supported by complex structures of enormous dimensions, influenced by the sumptuous style of the court of Bourdeaux, could be observed. The French fashion of wearing a *hennin*, a conical hat with a long flowing veil that descended down the back, had already been embraced in a previous period in Venice.

Giotto, *Ascencion of Saint John*, Florence, 1320

Monte di Bologna, *History of Saint Julien*, Trento, 1350-1360

SUMPTUARY LAWS

Starting at the end of the 13th century, the availability and variety of garments increased while awareness of the social role of clothing began to grow.

To balance old and new wealth, the requirement to regulate the use of garments with the aim of adapting one's daily life to societal changes emerged. In the 14th century, new sumptuary laws were issued that prohibited abuse and excessive ostentation of jewellery and adornments, establishing limitations on the amount of fabric used in clothes that regulated their width, length and other character-istics. These laws, fascinating documents about fashion in the past, stated, for example, that no one of lower rank than a baron could wear clothes made of velvet, carmine garments or attire embroidered in gold, nor could they use sable and ermine, as these were all signs of distinction reserved for those in power. Some important figures deplored the extravagant clothing and widespread exhibitionism of the period. Clergyman who preached moral values inspired by chastity and penitence condemned profligacy and the excessive interest in material things.

Taddeo Gaddi, *Saint Francis renounces worldly goods*, 1366

Women in a *hennin*, woman's headdress

Fashion in the 15th Century

HUMANISM AND THE FIRST ITALIAN RENAISSANCE

Giorgio Vasari, *Portrait of Lorenzo de Médici*, Florence 1533-1534

At the outset of the 15th century, humanism, an important cultural, literary and artistic phenomenon that place human beings at the centre of all things, emerged in Italy. In northern Italy, where strong courtly trends were maintained, the International Gothic current was weaker and was integrated into pre-existing artistic designs. The courts of Gonzaga in Mantua, Sforza and Visconti in Milan, Este in Ferrara, the republic of Venice and the court of Urbino under Federico II of Montefeltro flourished and prospered.

The Renaissance signified a cultural rebirth that sought to revitalise Greco-Roman classicism by giving a central place to reason. New mathematical knowledge disseminated in Europe by the Arabs, who expanded the Islamic world from India to Sicily and Spain, was incorporated. The epicentre of this large-scale revolution was the city of Florence, governed by the powerful and enlightened Medicis, a family of Tuscan bankers and businessmen. The court of Lorenzo de Medici represented for all of Europe a model of refinement in which the magnanimity of the patron, who surrounded himself with the best artists of the period, played a fundamental role in the modernisation of the architectural structures of places, piazzas, churches and gardens in an urban nucleus that over time became a rich and fertile international crossroads. The desire for beauty, along with technological evolution and the expansion of production, wed Italian good tastes and the expertise of talented artisans. The Renaissance extended from Italy to all of Europe, consolidating itself in various European courts. Artists of the period were adept at numerous disciplines, versatile masters that brought their ingenuity to a wide range of fields and enjoyed considerable social prestige. Leonardo da Vinci (1452-1519) was the prototype of the multifaceted artist. In his Codex Altanticus, he bequeathed to us many drawings accompanied by technical notes, the product of his inventive mechanical genius. Among these are raising and

Domenico Ghirlandaio, Tornabuoni Chapel, *Zacharias' naming of his son*, Florence, 1486-90

aligning machines to enhance wool fabrics, spindle twisters for continuous thread and blueprints for automatizing any sequence of movements on the loom. In the area of textile production, Leonardo worked on a punching machine, a device for manufacturing needles, another for producing *bizantini*, bright pieces similar to present day sequins, and others for making cords and trimming carpets. Responsible for organising court performances, he designed scenes, wardrobes and costumes for the "Feast of Paradise", in 1490, commissioned by Ludovico el Moro for the wedding of Gian Galeazzo Maria Sforza and Isabella of Aragon. In the middle of the 15th century, the Milanese silk industry experienced strong growth thanks to protected agreements between the Viscontis and Sforzas to favour the production of velvet, damask and silk as well as gold fabrics enriched with colourful silk. A mulberry tree (the favourite food of the silkworm) appeared on the personal shield of Ludovico, also known as "Ludovico il Moro" after the Milanese word *morone*, or "moor". The appearance of the first silk workers' association in Milan was documented in 1450. Silk fabric producers multiplied throughout Italy, and the courts in the rest of Europe took Italian style as a frame of reference, adopting its clothing and decorative fashions, thus benefitting the export of Italian fabrics. Antonio Pisanello (1394-1455), one of the major exponents of International Gothic in Italy, made studies of dressed figures depicted with a liberal wealth of details. His paintings document the use of the *balzo*, a typically Italian spherical woman's headpiece that revealed the plucked forehead, according to Flemish fashion.

Pisanello found inspiration in likenesses etched on coins and medals and painted distinguished members of the nobility in rigorous profile from nature. The beautiful details of the clothing call attention to the formidable financial resources of his clients. The portrait became the preferred medium for honouring people, and

Piero della Francesca, *Portrait of Battista Sforza*, 1465, Florence

Right: Ambrogio de Predis, *Portrait of a Lady*, *circa* 1485, Milan

Drawing by Pisanello

Right: Leonardo da Vinci, *Lady with Ermine*, 1488-90, Cracow

Pisanello, *Portrait of Lionello d'Este*, 1443,
Bergamo

Right: Antonio Pollaiolo, *Portrait of a Young
Lady*, 1470-1472, Milan

Carlo Crivelli, *Annunciation of Ascoli,* detail,
1486, London

Carlo Crivelli, *Madonna della Candeletta*, circa 1490, Milan

their moral qualities were highlighted through the representation of symbolic attributes. In the portrait of Lionello d'Este, Marquis of Ferrara, the foreground presents a rich brocade of gold thread with velvet borders on top of which large pearl buttons stand out. Women's hairstyles, inspired by the paintings of Botticelli, reached a high level of sophistication during the period and were enhanced with long strands of pearls and discriminating jewels held in place with ribbons, snoods and cloth tiaras. In some portraits by Piero della Francesca and Antonio del Pollaiolo, we can observe the use of pearl, whose glossy whiteness is an allusion to chastity. Other precious-stone accessories were necklaces, earrings, rings, shoulder buckles (for hooking the cloak) and waist buckles, the product of the most renowned goldsmithing and silversmithing of the period, resulting in enriching garments that were already sumptuous to begin with. Love of the harmony of forms moved from the realm of art into that of clothing, and artisanal luxury, reserved for a select few, became an export commodity that provided wellbeing and prosperity. Textile production was more uniform and articulated than in the past while the decorative trend of floral themes, evident in many pictorial representations from the Tuscan school, assumed a prominent place in fashion production. The products of high-end gold and silver work had always been used for religious devotion and worship. The embroidery on altar canopies was so exquisite that embroiderers were included in the professional category of metalsmiths. Fabric for tapestries, the board of which was always designed by painters, evolved considerably in Flanders, France and, later, Italy. Along with fabrics depicting figurative scenes (for liturgical use), the first designs signed by artists appeared.

In his later years, Jacobo Bellini, the Ferrara court painter, devoted himself to the study of textile decorations. Some of his designs have been preserved – sinuous motifs with stylized floral borders and Arabic calligraphy that foreshadowed the ogive mesh compositions that would later become fashionable. The increased precision of looms allowed for the production of smooth, bright velvet with a long or sheared pile, which required triple-thread silk. The veludieri, Venetian velvet manufacturers, specialized in this area, which included very expensive velvet cut at two heights and arranged on a background of gold and silver cloth. The pomegranate motif, symbol of fertility and abundance, appeared on the clothes of the

Madonne con Bambino by Carlo Crivelli as the inflorescence of the fruit inside a large leaf with a poly-lobed border. This motif of oriental origin became a favourite theme in Renaissance fabrics, expressed in a series of infinite variations with similar characteristics. Textile surfaces were enriched with thistle flowers, fan-palm flowers and tropical pineapples framed in large ogive leaves arranged in alternate horizontal sequences of voided velvet, which mimic metallic decorations, or in vertical sequences of sinuous bifurcated trunks. The artistic transformations introduced through architecture emphasised horizontal as opposed to vertical lines. The same designs appear on the fabrics used for tapestries and clothes, in ruby red, emerald green and lapis lazuli blue. The use of such highly ornate materials was justified as an affirmation of the merchant class that invested

Francesco del Cossa, *Saint Florian and Saint Lucia*, from the Griffoni polypytch, 1472-1473, Washington

large amounts of capital and made possible the circulation of rare and costly objects. It should be kept in mind that garments had a long shelf life and were even passed down from fathers to sons, such that their cost was amortised over time, with some modifications and repairs. Sleeves were the richest and most important element for determining the overall value of the garment. Accounting books and wills often mentioned fabrics that had been woven in precious metals and buttons with gem settings. The sumptuary laws continued to regulate luxury with standards that obligated certain social groups to bear only the distinctive signs of belonging to their class, though the laws were evaded and mocked through ploys and, more often than not, by paying the fines established for violators. In Bologna, a registry existed that approved the use of clothing each time the standards were updated, distinguishing not only the most minute fashion details but also summer and winter seasons. The changes reflected the shaping of forms, which gradually became more solid, resulting in a stiffer figure through a series of fillings made with all types of materials (sand, flour, rags, etc.). Particular emphasis was placed on the shoulders, chest and sides. The wardrobe of both sexes prescribed a series of strata of garments, with a layer lying tightly across the body defined as "tight garments to be worn underneath" (trouser-briefs, shirt and doublet for men; *gamurra* tightly across the breast, petticoat with flounces and saya for women) and ampler, more comfortable and refined clothes called "loose garments to be worn on top", often made of a series of stiff, triangular, structured pieces that outlined ideal anatomical forms. The dresses and layers of garments of both sexes had names such as clothes, *hopalanda*, *giornea*, Grenache, mantle, *lucco*, tabard. Footwear included slippers of varying heights, heels, clogs, leather or cloth *borzacchini* (high booties) and boots. Men's headwear, worn on top of long hair that fell to the neck and elegantly framed the face, was also quite varied.

Benozzo Gozzoli, *Procession of the Magi
(led by Lorenzo the Magnificent)*, 1459,
Florence

Andrea Mantegna, *The Court of Mantua*,
1471-74, Mantua

Details of medieval tapestries and silk fabric
from the same period

Fashion in the 16th century

Giovanni Battista Moroni, *Portrait of Isotta Brembati*, 1555, Bergamo

Jacopo Pontormo, *Portrait of Monsignor Giovanni della Casa*, circa 1550, Washington

THE EUROPEAN RENAISSANCE

Over the course the 16th century, a greater need for social control of behaviour evolved with the codification of "good manners" expressed through body language (postures, expressions, gestures and movements) and the representation of individual habits, among which clothing played an essential role. The 16th century saw the publication of diverse manuals and tracts that expressed rules of behaviour and offered advice and social norms that were learned and internalised for effective application. In 1528, Baldassarre Castiglione published the book of *the courtier,* a portrait of the perfect gentleman inspired by the values of the court life of Montefeltro of Urbino. The book extols, above all else, grace, an intimate virtue that expresses an elective condition based on birth and personal talent. In 1530 Erasmus of Rotterdam published de *civilitate morum puerilium*, a work aimed at children which contained observations regarding proper behaviour in church, at the table, in the bedroom and at play. The book quickly achieved great success because of its pedagogical approach and was translated into many European languages. In 1558, monsignor Giovanni della Casa (1503-56) published *il Galateo, overo de costumi*, the first proper etiquette manual that contained advice about how to converse, dress and behave in social life and contributed to reinforcing aristocratic privileges and the supremacy of appearances. The tract became so popular that the word *galateo* was incorporated into the Italian language to allude to the series of standards of behaviour identified with good manners. The "tailor's book", a beautiful collection of illustrations divided by types of sartorial designs and fashion figurines between 1540 and 1580, was also published in the 16th century. Books that presented types of clothing taken from real life served as a catalogue that enabled customers to choose the cut, fabric and adornments for the garments that they commissioned. In 1570 Giovan Battista Moroni underscored the importance of the tailoring profession, reserved for men, in a painting in which the artisan appears with a short white doublet, tightfitting and reinforced, in the "duck breast" style that became popular in the second half of the 16th century. With the discovery of America, the European economy received a strong expansionist boost that contributed new forms of wealth to the monarchies of nations.

Paolo Veronese, *The Madonna of the Cuccina Family*, circa 1571, Dresden

Designs from the "Tailor's Book II"
by Gian Giacomo Conte

In 1589-1590, venetian Cesare Vecellio published a compendium of cuts devoted to the types of garments known at the time. Entitled *Habiti antichi e moderni di tutto il mondo*, the work contained descriptions of the various types of clothing. During this period it is safe to assume that there was a veritable aesthetic revolution as for as women were concerned. Garments highlighted the female figure with fuller and curvier forms, widening the sides and emphasising the bust. The breasts, powdered and enhanced with makeup, expressed the fundamental qualities of a woman by virtue of their abundance, delicateness and softness. The skin was very white, subjected to lengthy exposures to moonbeams, while the ideal neck was svelte and the hands were fine and tapered.

Lorenzo Lotto, *Portrait of a Lady as Lucretia*,
1533, London

Giovanni Battista Moroni, *The Tailor*,
1565-70, London

Agnolo Bronzino, *Cosimo de' Medici*, 1537,
Saint Petersburg

Piero di Cosimo, *Mary Magdalene*, circa 1501,
Rome

Long blonde or "titian red" hair contrasted with scarlet lips and cheeks. To achieve this type of beauty, women in France relied on the iron corset, which fastened at the waist and went down in a point to the belly. Because of the danger it posed to the wearer, a lined corset supported by stiff wooden or metal rods soon replaced the iron corset. The breadth of the skirt was preserved at the sides of the body by a rigid bell-shaped structure *(pannier)* that reached down to the feet and contained filling. The legs were wrapped in tight breeches similar to those worn by men. The typical women's garment of the Renaissance after 1510 had broad, square shoulders, accentuated by a generous square neckline, with a slight enhancement in the centre. The breadth of the neckline varied according to age and social position (for instance, courtesans were often identified by a wide bateau neckline). The parts of the dress (corset and various hems of the skirt), joined to each other with little bows, left visible the candid whiteness of the undergarments, which showed through the neckline, skirts and sleeve fastenings. During the Renaissance, men and women's shirts of coarse linen, embroidered in cross-stitch or letters and either rust-coloured, blue or red, became widespread. The most elegant women of the period were Isabella d'Este, marquise of Mantua and wife of Francisco II Gonzaga; Beatrice d'Este; and Lucrecia Borgia, daughter of pope Alexander VI, who married Alfonso d'Este in a lavish ceremony and made her entry into Ferrara with seventy-two mules loaded with her personal belongings; Catalina de Medici, queen of France and wife of Henry II, who promoted Italian customs and fashions in the French court, where he introduced wide lace collars. Isabella d'Este was a fascinating, intelligent and highly cultivated woman, one of the most famous female personages of the century. Peopling the court of the Estes with scores of poets, writers and artists, she is remembered for having been the "source and origin of all the beautiful things of Italy" and wore shirts adorned with an enveloping floral border featuring figurative animal scenes. Similar designs, created in white or with threads of various colours, formed part of the wardrobes of important people and appear in the portraits painted by the most renowned artists of the period. In the painting *concerto*, by Callisto Piazza, a woman is wearing a white shirt with a neckline adorned with smocking embroidery technique that gathers the breadth of the fabric into pleats. Another very popular type of embroidery, executed in writing stitch on black silk, appears on the shirt of Simon George de Cornualles, whose portrait was painted by Bartolomeo Veneto, in Beatrice II d'Este (1510). Another dominant motif in embroidery designs in the 16th century were the *grotesques* in which little angles and "puttis" in face masks, mythological figures, trophies and laurel crowns alternating with fantastical animals appear. Sleeves, in a wide variety of styles, were much narrower while their confection and embroidery acquired more importance. They were always closed at the bottom to accentuate the horizontal line, puffy in the forearms and very tight in the cuffs, which at times extended as far as the fingertips. Around 1530 skirts opened in the front, from the waist to the selvedge, revealing the inner skirt. The *balzo*, a crescent-shaped headdress made of velvet adorned with bows and studded with gold and precious stones, or, alternatively, the hood, a circle of cloth that covered the forehead and head, with a strip that fell on the shoulders, were common. Another of the most beautiful and elegant ladies of the Italian Renaissance was Eleanor of Toledo, wife of Comiso de' Medici. One of her most spectacular dresses was cut from exquisite gold-work velvet with large arabesque drawings executed in an opulent and theatrical style of hispano-ar-

Hans Holbein the Younger, *Portrait of Thomas More*, 1527, Rome

Alessandro Allori, *Portrait of Eleanor of Toledo*, 1571, Vienna

Callisto Piazza, *Concert*, 1520-1530

Titian, *Portrait of Eleonora Gonzaga della Rovere*, 1536-1538, Florence

Right: Bartolomeo Veneto, *Beatrice II d'Este*, 1510, South Bend (USA)

Hans Holbein the Younger, *Portrait of Simon George de Cornualles*, 1535-1440, Frankfurt

abic influence. Eleanor would pass unnoticed through the piazzas of Florence, hidden in a green satin couchette the exterior of which was covered in velvet of the same colour. Among the preferred accessories of Renaissance ladies was the fan and the *pelliccia da pulci* (flea fur), a dissected animal, usually a skunk, weasel or sable, with the snout covered in gold and precious stones, which noble-women wore hanging from a gold chain to attract the parasites that infested domestic environments. Perfumed jewels that spread floral essences through the air and mitigated the most unpleasant odours compensated for the minimal attention commonly paid to personal hygiene. The most significant development in men's clothing was the introduction of more or less wide mid-thigh or knee-length breeches that formed a bulging covering at the sides, had lengthwise stripes and was worn over undergarment breeches; their length and width varied. At the beginning of the century, a small bag that was tied to the waist in the front, conceived as a pragmatic pocket, appeared. Toward the middle of the century, the bag transformed into the fly, a protuberant penile casing that extolled virile attributes. Breeches were reduced and held in place with garters and straps while shoes adopted the appearance of low square-toed "bear's feet" slippers. A tightfitting doublet, with a high collar, twisted and lined sleeves, wings on the shoulders and a short border instead of a skirt was worn over the shirt. Fitted in

Agnolo Bronzino, *Eleanor of Toledo with her son Giovanni*, 1545, Florence

Titian, *Charles V with a Dog*, 1533, Madrid

the waist, it ended in a point in the front and often was encircled by a metal belt from which the sword dangled. A small curled ruff that was repeated in the cuffs protruded from the collar. The most common hat was a velvet headdress, flat or cup shaped, that sat aslant with a curved feather and precious pin. The *shaube*, or german jacket, a garment with wide lateral cuts and puffy sleeves made of beautiful dense fabrics and lined with fur or a short round cape with purely decorative functions were worn over these garments. From the second half of the century on, printed textiles were re-sized. Large-size motifs with acanthus plants and heraldic symbols such as diamonds, suns, pears or caper flowers were replaced by small drawings of sprigs, commas, waves or bars with buds arranged in disorderly lines. The trend was toward simple, isolated and opposing elements; velvet on a satin background and damasks with brocade weaves were highly popular. Fashion was heavily influenced by the court of Charles I of Spain, a hegemonic catholic power and champion of the fight against the protestant reformers of Martin Luther whose numbers were increasing in nordic countries. Spanish noblemen wore their hair short with a moustache and sideburns and were fond of having their portraits painted in erect and bizarre postures dressed in rigid, lined garments that tended to be solemn and dark. The joining of the sleeves to the doublet was highlighted with borders adorned with festoon stitching, "picadillo" or "brahón". Women dispensed with collars, adopting stiffer skirts with the "verdugado", or farthingale, which

Silk and silver fabric with embossed motif emphasises with slits, 16th century

gave them a conical shape and hid the volumes of the figure completely. Black was the prevailing colour, and sumptuous adornments and dense embroidery in gold with a profusion of beautiful buttons and pins abounded. While some common features were preserved, the european wardrobe ultimately reflected the cultural and ideological connotations of each country. Although it adopted bright colours such as yellow and red, german attire was distinguished by a sense of parsimony as opposed to an abundance of fabric and by a moderate employment of decorative elements predominant in other countries. Women's clothing reflected as evolution in gothic style, although the waist was highlighted and narrowed with a corset that cinched below the breasts. Sleeves, falling from the

Alonso Sánchez Coello, *Don Carlos, Prince of Austria*, 1558, Madrid

Lorenzo Lotto, *Lucina Brembati*, 1518, Bergamo

shoulders, became puffy at the elbow and had funnel-shaped cuffs. Broad starched snoods held place with metal objects and fastened to the neck with bands and subtle nylon strips, were worn on the head. The main innovation was in the style of the *slashes* made in dresses in order to reveal the fabrics underneath. It is said that this originated in nantes because of an episode of war in which the Swiss army, after defeating the troops of charles the bold, sacked the tents and silk materials that duke of Bordeaux always took with him, even in battles. After cutting the precious fabrics into shreds, they used them to fashion their own clothes. The custom of cutting precious fabrics to call attention one's superiority was initially adopted by the Swiss mercenaries but later became a widespread custom and was regarded as a symbol of power in many circles, to the point that many designs of breeches and doublets from the period were made by joining long cut strips of material together and place one alongside the other. *Los abullonados* that reveal strips of white clothing or lining of contrasting colours multiplied and spread everywhere. In England, the attire that the Tudors chose to wear spotlights the wealth of the nation, which underwent a period of strong economic development thanks to trade. Elizabeth I promoted lavish luxury as an external manifestation of her role as a magnanimous queen. Sleeves acquired

Alonso Sánchez Coello, *Portrait of Infante Ferdinand of Spain*, 1575, Baltimore, USA

William Scrots, *Elizabeth I when a Princess*, 1546, London

Alonso Sánchez Coello, *Isabel Clara Eugenia and Magdalena Ruiz*, 1586, Madrid

G. B. Moroni, *The Black Knight*, 1567, Milan

the grotesque form of hams; starched lace collars were pleated in openwork ruffs that encircled the head like gigantic aureoles. The skirt, held in place by a metal hoop, acquired the shape of a small round table with a heater underneath, concealing the body completely. Embroidery with pearls and jewels adorned ceremonial suits. French Renaissance fashion was dominated by Catalina de Medicis, regent of her three children after the death of Henry II. Catalina adopted widow's snoods and collars adorned with lace, opened in corollas and high, and introduced Florentine used and garments into the French court. The very narrow waist, artificially deformed from the bust, remained popular for all European ladies.

Fashion in the 17th Century

BAROQUE PERIOD

In the first decades of the 17th century, Europe suffered a series of political and social convulsions as a result of the rivalry between Catholics and Protestants that would lead to the devastating Thirty Years' War (1618-1648). The Spanish empire rapidly lost political and military prestige under the threat of England, Holland, Portugal and France, which embarked on the colonisation of the Americas.

Upon the death of Charles I of England, the Commonwealth imposed a Puritan regime that frowned upon the ostentation of wealth.

In Holland, the Protestant middle class gained control of the state and became the protagonist of an extraordinary period of prosperity in the fields of commerce and the arts. The adoption of a puritanical way of life by the most important European nations produced rapid transformations in Renaissance fashion. During this period of transition, styles evolved quickly and acquired local connotations derived from the governing courts of emerging states such as Sweden, Prussia and Russia, where all of the aristocracy

Aztec attire

Anton van Dick, *Lord John Stuart and his brother Bernard*, 1638, London

Frans Hals, *Catharina Hooft with Her Nurse*, 1620, Berlin

Anton van Dick, *Young King Charles II of England with his spaniel, circa* 1639, London

Below: Gian Lorenzo Bernini, bust of Thomas Baker, 1638, London

gathered. The cult of refinement and good manners, inherent in the desire to rise and prove oneself in economic, artistic and cultural circles, extended to the wealthy merchant middle class and their children, whose style of dress was not very different from that of the privileged nobility, though the fabrics were less exclusive.

For the first time, the word moda (fashion), from *modus*, appeared, suggesting a style of life and clothing in a wider sense that extended to many aspects of existence, not only garments. In the 17th century, a taste for baroque aesthetics, characterised by surprising scenic and theatrical effects embodied in the fusion of architecture, sculpture and painting, flourished in Europe. Abandoning classical rigour, artists embraced a style that venerated the curved line and a profusion of details and developed malleable compositional rhythms obtained by alternating chiaroscuro effects.

Occasionally using repetitive compositional structures that included optical illusions, mirrors, cases and golden horns, decorations and clothing assumed sumptuous forms that promoted high quality artisanal work and inventiveness applied to the enhancement of the male and female wardrobe through the use of diverse accessories: feather fans, ties and lace adornments, embroidered velvet gloves and mittens, exquisite silk footwear and large curled wigs.

Anton van Dick. *Maria Louisa de Tassis*, *circa* 1630, Liechtenstein

Woman's shoe, late 17th century

In the first decades of the century, Spanish tastes, typical of the hegemonic Catholic monarchy, which adopted a stiff and dour style of dress, remained predominant. Slight changes were introduced to alleviate the cumbersomeness of fillings and make garments looser so as to better facilitate movement, in keeping with a certain vigorousness favoured by Baroque aesthetics. Men's breeches gradually became longer and narrower, adorned with buttons and rosettes at the sides. Breeches, black and white, were made of mesh and extended far enough down to cover the legs.

A more practical collar, the *golilla*, substituted the uncomfortable ruffs. Golden lace cuffs that protruded from narrow contoured sleeves remained popular. Hairstyles, short or long above the ears, included thin curled sideburns and the characteristic goatee on the chin. Capes became longer and wider.

The middle of the century saw a resurgence of the woman's dress divided into two pieces. Spanish women adopted a wide bateau décolleté covered by a more or less transparent shawl collar. Sleeves were shortened; softer and puffier, they were joined to the shoulders at a lower point and adorned with fillings, bows, braids and passementerie edges, like on the hems of petticoats. The bodice was refined with a triangular point and skirts were

Diego Velázquez, *Maria Ana of Austria*, 1652-1653, Madrid

REPRESENTATION OF POPULAR CLOTHING

Johannes Vermeer, *The Milkmaid*,
1658-1660, Amsterdam

During these years, along with the opulent and ostentatious clothing of the ruling class, images of ordinary men and women engaged in daily activities and exhibiting realistic expressions and characteristics appeared.

Pieter Brueghel the Elder had already depicted the motley world of daily existence with realism and irony, capturing in the ungainly profiles of kitchen helpers, patrons of taverns and beggars, the authentic common spirit of tradition. The Peasant Dance and The Peasant Wedding (1565-66) represent two moments of celebra-tion in which the clothing of the poor does not lack colour. Joachim Beuckelaer, a genre painter of the Antwerp school, captures the lively atmosphere of an outdoor scene in The Fish Market (1574), where the pinkish colours of common clothing balance the sharp and carnal light of the food in baskets, symbolic of an acquired wealth. The garments, depicted in their natural context, speak of the human condition, feelings and emotional states of the people wearing them, in a physical narration that does not require words.

lengthened with wide contoured canesù. Oval-shaped skirts were held in place with a "tambour" verdugado that was flat in the front and back centre and widened considerably at the sides.

In 1602 the Dutch created the East India Company for the purpose of importing to Europe, through the ports of Amsterdam and Antwerp, all sorts of exotic consumer goods accessible in distant colonial realms. Emporiums and warehouses were opened in India, Japan, Ceylon and Siam, local hubs for goods that were loaded onto ships and which provided rapid economic development to the country. The Dutch reflected the dignity and pride of social belonging in their dark clothing, which adopted a comfortable and curvilinear "barrel" shape, always enlivened with white linen collars that rested on the shoulders in the form of soft, flat fans and quickly replaced the stiff starched ruffs with a mill wheel shape.

Women's attire reflected acquired wealth and used an abundance of fabric in overlapping skirts.

To give more volume to the buttocks, a leather circle that was tied to the waist and provided internal support was adopted. The preferred fabrics were iridescent satins and silk, of plain colours or with small motifs. Lace rosettes and ribbons constituted the ornamentation of the *vlieger*, a dress-cape with puffy sleeves that reached to the ground. In keeping with the prevailing Calvinist moral code, precious stones and ostentatious jewellery were eschewed. During those years, Johannes Vermeer painted Girl with Turban (also called Girl with a Pearl Earring) and The Lacemaker. Hairstyles were simple; the hair was gathered in tightfitting snoods that highlighted the roundness of the face. Men's attire consisted of a

Lavinia Fontana, *Family portrait*, 1613, Milan

Right: Orazio Gentileschi, The Lute Player, 1624, Washington

PREFERENCE FOR THE COLOUR BLACK

The documented use of black clothing such as mourning garments dates back to 1419 in the Duchy of Burgundy, when Duke Philip the Good adopted them permanently to express his grief over the assassination of his father by the French. The sophisticated court of Burgundy instilled in this colour an aristocratic and solemn tone capable of embodying the distinctive nature of power. There were different shades of black: "true black", of the highest quality, was obtained with iron powder from sword filings; other black tones tended toward green or brown, or they were pinker or darker, obtained with barbs or tannins, and were resistant to alterations over time. In the textile sphere, black dye was the most expensive and hardest to obtain, requiring successive colour baths that tended to corrode the structure of the fibre. The Protestant

Reformation led by Martin Luther, which opposed to the degeneration of tradition on the part of the Roman Catholic Church, adopted black as the ideological colour that annihilated earthly vanity in one stroke and directed attention to fundamental principles and values. In the 16th century, alongside the bright, contrasting and varied colours in the Renaissance gentleman's wardrobe, dark colours, recommended as a sign of distinction by Baldassarre Castiglione in his celebrated work The Courtier, gained prominence. The austere Spanish court of Charles V adopted black as an emblem of stringent morality and imposed it as the official colour of ceremonial garments required by standards of etiquette. In response to the ostentatious abundance of decorations that the sumptuary laws fecklessly sought to combat, the fashion for plain cloth, silk damask, and compact black satin, a notion of renunciation and

humility that posited the value of a masculine image that highlighted bravery in battle and virtuous behaviour emerged. Black velvet, also used by women, was highly appreciated for its characteristic brightness and was a speciality of the city of Genoa, which remained the irrefutable leader of the luxury fabrics market for many years. The colour black became a symbol of institutions during the gradual transition from religious values to those of the emerging capitalism spreading all over Europe. In the 17th century, merchants, doctors and judges in northern Europe began to wear garments made of solemn and opaque black fabrics. Particularly in the Netherlands, these colours expressed the middle class work ethic, industriousness in business and rigorous respect for the law. At the beginning of the 17th century, with the general evolution of society and the recognition of new collective and professional identities, the pictorial genre of the group portrait experienced a resurgence.

Thomas de Keyser, *Members of the civilian guard of Amsterdam's 11th district under the command of Captain Allart Cloeck*, 1632, Amsterdam

Rubens, *Hélène Fourment with Children*, *circa* 1636, Paris.

VERMEER'S LACEMAKER

The Lacemaker (1669-1670) by Johannes Vermeer depicts a scene from daily life set in a 17th-century middle class Dutch interior. The woman is focused on making lace with the help of needles in a stuffed cushion around which thin white threads passed through two fine wooden bones that she manages with her hands are interwoven. In the foreground, on the table, is a workbox covered in velvet and decorated with tassels from which bunches of white and red thread protrude. Lace, an allusion to the feminine virtues of patience and laboriousness, constituted an important source of income for ordinary women as an activity performed in the home.

The woman's face – serious and absorbed in her work – is framed in a typical hairstyle of the period. A horizontal line divides the mass of hair gathered in a braided bun. Two side ringlets brush against the temples and are collected in twisted, wavy points. The woman is wearing a golden yellow dress with a white linen "baby" collar open in the front. Bobbin lacework was very widespread in Flanders and the Netherlands, particularly in Malinas, Binche, Bruges and Brussels, where a type of highly appreciated linen, of inimitable whiteness and fineness, abounded. Prized by nobles of both sexes as an adornment on collars and cuffs, it was adopted by the wealthy European bourgeoisie.

Michiel Jansz van Mierevelt, *George Villiers, Duke of Buckingham*, 1625, North Terrace (Australia)

Johannes Vermeer, *Girl with Turban*, 1665, The Hague

doublet that buttoned in the front, with skirts of various lengths, similar to an off-the-shoulder dress coat, and which was worn over knee-length breeches closed with eye-catching rosettes.

Men's shoes, adorned with buckles or bows, had a lance-shaped point and high heels. Often breeches reached down to the thigh-high bootleg, cut in funnel shapes and worn loose with the upper part folded over. Sleeves, which were increasingly wide and left the white shirt below visible, were added to the bust with numerous knotted bows. In the second half of the 17th century, Dutch men did not hesitate to adopt the *Rhingrave* (from the Dutch *Rijn Gra* he shoulders, and tall black felt hats with a squat conical crown and a wide, stiff rim were common. In the 17th century, Italian tastes and styles were not as overwhelming as they were during the Renaissance, and the influence of Spanish dominance diminished in the realm of fashion as well.

The most requested fabrics were velvet with alternating sprig or bouquet motifs, which were also executed on less dense fabrics, on satin or damask with a polychrome weave, on green velvet for decorating, on floral satin embroidery, and many other types of solid colour bases. Milan, Genoa, Venice, Florence and Naples were the most active centres, exporting a significant part of their own production.

The Duchy of Milan, which in the past had specialised in the production of gold-embroidered silk fabrics and other kinds of embroidery, gradually moved toward the raising of silkworms and the semi-manual production of yarns. Master weavers abandoned the intense activity of the loom, obtaining significant benefits by immigrating to France. The republic of Venice maintained important contacts with all the cities in northern Europe and continued to exert its political and economic influence through vibrant trade relations with Asia, threatened by incursions by the Turks.

"Colour vendors", international merchants that had wide ranges of colours obtained from pigments as well as ingredients to produce dye formulas for fabrics, were active in Venice. The aristocratic class, for its part, embraced the new vogue for "middle dyes". Intermediate and defused colours, they began to be used in Italy, constituting one of the most significant innovations at the time insofar as they distanced themselves from bright, saturated colours and adopted pink, powdery, bluish, faded, greyish, straw-coloured and iridescent tones. Middle dyes required less colouring material, almost invariably imported from India or the Americas, and less tonal immersions in baths. They were easier to acquire, more economical than intense Renaissance dyes and, thus, more suitable for garments that were changing more often, according to the whims of fashion.

In the second half of the century, French fashion, supported and promoted by the long-term economic policies of the state managed by Cardinal Richelieu, his secretary Mazzarino and Minister Colbert, who was not above industrial espionage and who hired Venetian and Italian lace makers for the French court, was enthusiastically reaffirmed. These efforts sought to legitimize the consumption of domestic luxury and the unquestionable dominance of France over the rest of Europe. Under the reign of Louis XIV, the Sun King, the French nobility lived in the palace at Versailles and led an ostentatious and profligate life of parties, pageants, outings, concerts, masquerades, dances and theatrical and pyrotechnical performances. The most talented artists of the period, such as, for instance, Charles Lebrun, were hired not only as portrait painters that documented an existing reality but also as makers and creators with direct responsibilities in the organisation and supervision of aesthetic manifestations related to the sovereign and his entourage.

Justaucorp and rhingrave were the preferred garments of men, complemented by heeled shoes and wigs that accentuated a style replete with ribbons, one that was contrived, ostentatious and unmanly. In 1670 men's wardrobes stabilised around the suit jacket with long skirts, sleeves with ample cuffs, a shirt worn below and tight breeches, closed at the knee, called *coulottes*.

Charles Le Brun, *Chancellor Sèguier*, 1661, Paris

BAROQUE HAIRSTYLES

The "Fontange" coiffure owes its fortune to a casual episode in which Madeimoselle de Fontanges, a favourite of Louis XIV whose hair had become tousled during a hunting expedition, rearranged her abundant locks using a band adorned with lace and bows. Amused by this stroke of ingenuity, the Sun King expressed his appreciation of the unusual hairstyle soon imitated by all French ladies, who were responsible for its spectacular popularity between 1680 and 1715.

The French-style suit appeared, complemented by thin breeches of white or coloured silk, a beautiful sash tied at the side, lace ties knotted at the neck and leather muffs. Women's dresses defined a more slender silhouette again. The upper part, close-fitting thanks to a corset, extended along an embroidered shirtfront and left the neck and neckline free. The sleeves reached down to the elbow; part of the arm, on which wide fringes of light lace called *engageantes* fell, was left bare. A type of skirt with a tail, called *mantello*, made of satin or silk-lined velvet, with adorned or hooked borders, was sewn to the corset. Below was the skirt per se, of plain colour, with horizontal fringe or composite drawings, produced in Lyon factories. An apron with a shirtfront was often added to provide grace to garments. Paris was the centre of the world, and everyone wanted to emulate the magnificence of a whimsical and elitist lifestyle. French manufacturers sold their goods everywhere while the dynamic succession of new garments gave rise to the phenomenon of fashion as we know it today.

Italian ladies in Baroque dresses

Fashion in the
18th Century

FROM BAROQUE TO ROCOCCO

In the 17th century, French style foisted itself decisively onto the international scene. Europe and America continued looking to France as the indisputable arbiter of elegance. Until then, fashion had been known primarily through drawings of figurines published in selections of engravings: Recueil des modes by Roger Gaignères (1570-1580), Les grands seigneurs by Jacques Callot (1617) and Le jardin de la noblesse française by Abraham Bosse (1633). At the end of the 17th century, the French garment market was in a state of complete transformation. As fashion cycles became shorter and clothing styles began to change at a faster pace, the *Mercure Galant* (1672-74), the first urban French newspaper aimed at a wide public, appeared. Fashion continued to be limited to the social elite, who were distinguished by their manner of dress and immortalised in stiff poses in the portraits of contemporary artists. The king was

Pietro Longhi, *The Dancing Lesson*, 1741, Venice

Jean Antoine Watteau, *Halt During the Hunt*, 1720, Paris

a human idol in whose presence even science showed deference. The garments of nobles, clergyman and military officials were adorned with embroidery, elaborate borders and feathers. While merchants differentiated themselves from artisans and serfs, the differences between aristocrats and the bourgeoisie were less marked, as society in general was more open to changes. The range of ever-changing colours to choose from grew. The enlightened ideas of Montesquieu, Voltaire and Rousseau prepared society to embrace a new mentality, one based on freedom of thought and action. Meanwhile, to safeguard their rank and maintain their ancient acquired privileges, nobles and well-born men and women continued to pay meticulous attention to personal care, allowing themselves to be seduced by excess and indulging in intricate artifices. In Paris, female seamstresses, until then subordinate to men, obtained official recognition (1675) and formed the association of *Maitresses Couturières*, though they were only authorised to dress people of their own gender for obvious reasons of modesty. Starting in 1730, they could also produce whalebone corsets and full bras that acquired considerable significance. Along with the *lingères*, devoted to production of undergarments, new professions emerged that specialised in clothing accessories, adornments and small complements that acted in close contact with tailors and fabric suppliers. Around the middle of the century, the Encyclopaedia of Diderot and D'Alembert was published.

François Boucher, *The Modiste*, 1746, London

This work contained detailed etchings of the development of artisanal activities and the tools used in the practical professions that represented a resource for society's poorest members. In the first decades women's clothing widened in the back in the shape of a trapezoid, with long lengthwise pleats called "Watteau pleats" (because they were prominent in the artist's work) which began at the neck and extended down the back, forming a tail.

This style corresponded to a single-piece dress. It had a square neckline, was made of soft silk fabric of pale, watercolour tones and was called robe volant (floating dress). It was complemented

Jean Antoine Watteau, *The Shopsign of Gersaint*, 1720, Berlin

Example of *andrienne*

ANDRIENNE

The *andrienne* consisted of an inner skirt replete with festooned adornments and a cloak-dress with a plunging V-shaped neckline open in front and which closed only at the waist in the "pièce d'estomac", a triangular front piece that was always profusely decorated. In the front, the dress had narrow shoulders and a cinched bodice while in back deep pleats extended to the ground without attaching to the chest, forming a kind of a cloak with a tail. Inspired by the chamber clothing that Madame de Montespan, the lover of Louis XIV, wore during her numerous pregnancies, the andrienne led to the flourishing of the farthingale, a support that granted the skirt a characteristic bell shape. Its width also justifies the description *robe négligé*, a generic term applied to comfortable and simple household or travel garments. The tight sleeves encompassed the arm, ending in a funnel shape.

18TH CENTURY BUST

Women tended to project a fragile and genteel image, the result of the enormous sacrifice that they had to make to endure the torture of the corset. The wasp waist remained a fundamental requirement of 18th century fashion emphasised progressively by the development of the internal forms of fastening the skirt. The constrictive corset with a stiff central iron bar (or of wood, mother-of-pearl or silver) used in the 17th century was abandoned in favour of ones composed of a large number of whalebone, which were flexible and subtle, aligned and inserted between two sewn stitches. The prevailing lifestyle was not as moderate. To the contrary, it stimulated licentious behaviour and libertine habits, more or less clandestine encounters of lovers that required adequate garments, ones capable of exalting fascination and personal charm.

To achieve slenderness and emphasise the bust, which was no longer squeezed down but attached upwards, two types of bras were adopted: one incorporated directly in the dress and another that was an indepenedent intimate garment. Both types were also used simultaneously. The inner bra was always of sewn cloth, while the outer version was made with fine fabrics such as satin, damask, chintz, in some cases the same as that of the dress. They fastened in the front or back, or in some cases both, with eyelets through which braid or ribbons passed to regulate pressure.

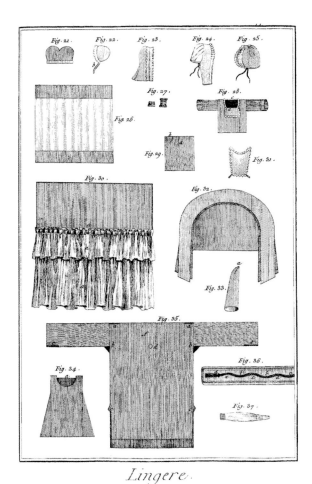

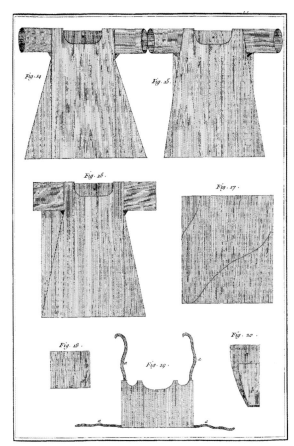

Lingere.

Lingere 2.

Ilustrations from the *Encyclopeadia of Diderot and D'Alembert*

by a hairstyle characterized by curls gathered in a ribbon that left the nape of the neck completely bare. Later, the model evolved into a two-piece dress and took the name of *andrienne*, after the protagonist of a comedy performed in Paris in 1703. Initially considered a comfortable and informal garment worn over the breasts, the *andrienne* was gradually embraced as the "court" dress and its unique structure was the basis for defining the most representative female garment of the century: the robe à la française used in ceremonies and which, due to its elaborate network of fastenings, required complex series of operations to put on.

The first pannier, stiff circles made of hemp or whalebone that girded and extended the width of skirts, began to appear in 1718. Around the middle of the century, the pannier divided into two sections, one for each side, that tied with a ribbon. Their sizes grew to the point where women had to turn to the side to pass through doors. The sleeves adopted the *pagoda* form, an expression of the unbridled passion for anything Chinese. The exotic and extravagant, the unusual and unknown were appropriated for the simple reasons that these curiosities diminished the boredom of everyday life.

Fabrics consisting of large patches were used both for decoration and in the clothing of both sexes. Garments acquired certain vibrancy due to the presence of large damasked surfaces enriched with polychromatic brocade weaves of gold and silver threads.

In designs produced in the factories of Lyon, patterns of oriental influence were among the most popular, thanks to the unusual union of sinuous floral elements with objects of falsified propor-

THE PANNIER

Two ladies from the court of Louis XV conceived of the pannier to conceal their obesity in their lower regions. Through the application of a rigid support (at first discreet and later more extensive), either round, elliptical, downward or raised, it was possible to construct an artificial shape that was superimposed on the natural constitution of the body. During the time of Louis XVI, the pannier was divided into two authentic baskets placed at the sides in such a way that the skirt, when expanding, allowed air to circulate. Very high panniers, constructed almost at a right angle, were also called "elbow pannier" because the arms could be rested on them. In the second half of the 18th century, large panniers were used only on ceremonial dresses, disappearing for good around 1780.

English-style dress, 1780

Francois Boucher, *Madame de Pompadour*,
1756, Munich

tions, to the point that they earned the epithet of "bizarre" fabrics.

Weavers from other countries were quick to imitate Lyons fabrics. Baroque style evolved into more inflamed forms on account of interwoven decorative elements that simulated lace structures, leather, elegant undulating ribbons, shells, sylvan landscapes, gazebos, pagodas and ruins. Flights of fancy were expressed on delicate surfaces of the body through curves and picturesque elements.

Rococco style remained predominant for a large part of the 17th century. It is characterised by fantastical adornments distributed throughout the garment, particularly on the front. Madame Pompadour's favourite ones often featured a ladder of ribbons.

During the reign of Louis XV, the *caraco*, a somewhat long jacket, was adopted, while rare animal furs and hooded capes became fashionable.

In 1785 the "robe à l'anglaise", a more linear garment, which had a kind of cuff below the kidneys and consisted primarily of light fabrics in elegant pastel tones, appeared. Because of its simplicity, the "robe à l'anglaise" lent itself as well to production in muslin and stamped cotton fabrics, another major innovation of the time that would later become extremely popular in neoclassical society.

Pompeo Batoni, *Francis Basset*, 1778, Madrid

While all women wore muslin neckerchiefs and shirtfronts, the fabrics and adornments used were distinguished depending on the occasion and social roles. Around 1710 the word *abito* appeared. The term referred to men's basic clothing, which consisted of a dress coat (in French, *justacorps*), a knee-length fitted jacket with sleeves and funnel-shaped cuffs fastened with buttons and horizontal pockets with profiled flaps; a gilet, a kind of vest slightly shorter than a jacket that buttoned in the front and had long, narrow sleeves; and tight breeches. This combination, influenced by military attire, was always made of beautiful fabrics and outlined with braids and golden passementerie. The individual elements of the "suit a la francaise" evolved over time with modifications in the cut, proportions and length.

During the Regency era (1715-1723) shoulders became narrower and the jacket assumed the name *marsina*, after the Count De Marsin, a French general. Characterised by long skirts and lined with waxed cloth to give more breadth to the sides, the marsina was bell-shaped and full with five or six large pleats that spread out on both sides, creating an ideal correspondence with the pannier.

The central set of buttons was purely decorative, as the marsina was always worn open. Buttons acquired a very costly appearance, including gold filigree, passementerie and the composition of the embroidery worked "à la disposition" of polychrome silk and covered with embroidered fabric as well.

The vest was the "sotto-marsina", which lost the sleeves and was enriched with lovely embroidery on satin backgrounds of moire or velvet, which acquired a life of its own. Not necessarily cut from the same fabric as the jacket, it was worn meticulously buttoned. Gradually the sottomarsina became increasingly shorter, eventually acquiring the appearance of the present-day vest.

During the reign of Louis XV, the marsina became shorter and the sleeves were reduced, opening up space for vests with vaporous and frizzy lace, while breeches now extended below the knee. Shoes with heels were embellished with rectangular metal buckles and bejewelled rosettes. In the first half of the century (1728), the *redingote*, a woman's long coat that crossed over the chest, appeared (the name comes from "riding coat".) At the end of the century, it replaced the cape and from 1785 on was also worn by women while preserving the distinctive features of a masculine garment.

At this time, an alternative to the marsina appeared, the frock coat, a fitted garment without buttons or pockets and considered less formal, which would achieve great popularity by the end of the century. The reign of Loius XVI saw a return to simplicity; widths were reduced and sleeves lengthened. The clothing of servants and domestic workers also acquired certain significance insofar as they revealed the way of life of their masters. Valets, footmen, porters and coachmen wore special uniforms (livery) made of durable and resistant materials adorned with braids and other passementerie.

Common people and artisans wore breeches, shirts and short vests cut from very simple, economical fabrics. The women wore corsets, skirts, camisoles, aprons and neckerchiefs but not intimate apparel.

People who performed more lowly tasks as well as peasants dressed like servants and wore wooden clogs.

Far removed from the squalor of the lower classes, considered mere instruments of the well being of the court, the nobility and high clergy maintained a life of luxury and overindulgence, characterised by vain and artificial pursuits. The volume of their wigs reached such enormous proportions that they became the most striking symbol of social inequality. When the winds of revolution brought the crystallization of new ideals, the heads covered in powdered white wigs would be the first to fall in the guillotine.

The French Revolution of 4 July 1789, inspired by the principles of "liberty, equality and fraternity", did away with royal despotic power and abolished, above all, privileges in dress, imposing dark, unadorned clothing for men and forbidding women, for a period of time, from using corsets, puffy petticoats, powders and high heels.

On a print from 1791, the likeness of "Liberty, Patron of the French" wears a Phrygian cap, the symbol of slaves liberated from ancient Rome, while sumptuous tri-coloured ribbons are used to tie the booklets of documents presented to the National Assembly. The garments used to provide uniformity acquired an explicit political function, transmitting ideological principles and values. Cockades

Gian Domenico Tiepolo, *Family Meal*, Villa Valmarana (Vicenza, Italy), 1757

George Morland, *The Stable Door*, 1790, London

and hats, used for certain events, became legally codified emblems.

The prevailing severity during the period of the Estates General imposed a rigid, British-influenced notion of fashion that was quickly embraced as the official outfit by the new representatives of the people. Frock coats and redingotes were dark and made of plain fabrics. They were paired with long, tight breeches tucked into the boots and white shirts whose collar was closed by a wide tie knotted like a shawl around the chin. People who continued to wear expensive silk clothing were included in an index and considered enemies of the Revolution.

The *sans-culotte* (without culottes) wore the *carmagnole* jacket, a shapeless *justacorps* of coarse fabric that reached the knee with long, wide pants with a three-button horizontal cover. Revolutionary attire was completed with a white shirt, striped vest and neckerchief. The Titus cut, or "coiffure a la victime" hairstyle, was also popular at the time.

The passion for new republican ideals revitalised an interest in ancient Greco-Roman attire. As shirts and petticoats were forbidden, elegant women wore old-style tunics. Clinging garments, they fastened below the barely hidden breasts, left the arms bare and opened below the knee. During the Reign of Terror, the *merveilleuses* were covered only with transparent veils, like Greek goddesses, which resulted in their frequently catching cold. Under the tunic they wore a flesh-coloured silk "maglia da corpo".

Merveilleuses

Jacques Louis David, *People's Representative
of the Armies*, 1790, Paris

From Court Dress
to 19th Century
Bourgeois Fashion

NAPOLEONIC ERA (1796-1815)

French Empire style, which made an appeal to the purity of a classical figure magnifying a glorious destiny, became established in all of Europe as a vibrant attitude officially launched on the day of Napoleon and his wife Josephine's coronation, on 2 December 1804. Jean-Baptiste Isabey, ultimately serving as a mirror for the entire era, studied the ornamental fabrics and the dress designs worn in the lavish ceremony by kings and queens, ambassadors, marshals and dignitaries, all portrayed in Jacques-Louis David's *The Coronation of Napoleon*, with choreographic premeditation. A complex court machinery governed official and fashionable affairs, where the protocol of strict etiquette and the new "bon genre" rules increased the inventory of fabrics, enriched by new materials such as tulle, muslin and crepe from China and securing numerous orders for the luxury industries. The Napoleonic conquests in Egypt had contributed to archaeological research that influenced art, culture, clothing and adornments. Women's dresses expressed an elegant simplicity: a long shirt with a feint tail, a generous neckline and short, puffy sleeves that highlighted a snow-white bust. The silhouette was light and vertical, defined by a closefitting bust (from then on known as "Empire style"), suggesting the image of the vestal virgins of ancient Greece. The lightness of the muslins and veils allowed for a transparent view of the human figure.

For court dresses, to create more consistency, the fabric of choice was ivory satin with embroidered hems. Palms, acanthus leaves, flower crowns and bouquets were the most used motifs. On top of the dress, a cape-coat open at the front was worn. The ensemble was completed with long, fitted gloves and precious rectangular

Marie-Guillemine Benoist, *Portrait of Pauline Bonaparte*, 1807, Versailles

Jacques-Louis David, *The Coronation of Napoleon*, 1805, Paris

woollen shawls with cashmere motifs. The curled up-do hairstyle also drew inspiration from Greco-Roman style. Men adopted the English style, consisting of a dress coat with long tails made of dark cloth or velvet and large cuffs, fitted breeches inserted in the boots or reaching the knee and revealing the stockings. The vest had a low neck, leaving room for a necktie looped twice and tied with an ample knot that covered the chin. The redingote was the coat commonly used, while a walking cane and a black cylindrical hat were the most common accessories. The emperor was not alien to the charms of fashion: he owned 48 gala outfits and many more of other types adequate for the different circumstances of imperial life. He had his initials embroidered in gold and used to wear lace neckties, which he imposed as an accessory of the court dress of high dignitaries. He took charge of the recovery of refined textile manufactures and promoted the latest innovations for the manufacture of engraved fabrics obtained with the punched card system devised by Joseph Marie de Jacquard (1752-1834), from Lyon.

Jean-Baptiste Wicar, *Portrait of Murat*, 1810, Lille

Anne-Louis Girodet, *Portrait of Chateaubriand*, 1810

THE BOURBON RESTORATION (1814-1831)

During the Bourbon Restoration, the disappearance of Napoleonic ideals also saw the departure of coloured uniforms. Men's clothes went through a period of change, tending toward practicality and restraint, characteristic of Lord Brummel's English elegance. Affluent men choose civilian clothes that were simple and well tailored, made of woollen fabrics of extremely subdued colours: olive green, oil, brown, grey, blue and black. The tailcoat remained popular. It had fitted sleeves, long tails, a stand-up collar, large cuffs and gold buttons, and would eventually become a garment reserved for ceremonies. Trousers were fitted, often with vertical stripes, and were worn tucked into loose and slouchy boots or ones that were elongated like soft tubes. During the winter, the redingote, an informal, sporty, cross-button garment worn in the countryside that represented an evolution in the riding coat, was the preferred crossover jacket. On top of it, wide-sleeved overcoats were adopted as well as capes. Men's shirts acquired a touch of frivolity with frills and tucks. Noteworthy was the white embroidered silk necktie. The vest helped to provide shape to the torso: a collar with wedges, in pique, cashmere or suede, and also used dually, overlapping a white one with another one in colour. This masculine outfit became the image that best expressed the characteristics of the heterogeneous bourgeoisie, increasingly aware of its social role. Any bare part of a woman's body was covered, constituting the absolute triumph of the sense of decency. French women appeared wrapped in high-collared dresses made from a single conical cut, with the skirt having up to three layers of pleated frills or decreasing and repeated hems. The sleeves were long and fitted, while the waist, initially high, gradually lowered itself to its natural position. Hats, bonnets and tall hats with feathers, short, light kidskin gloves, muffs and leather embellishments were the most highly sought after accessories. Around 1820, France produced tulle with the warp loom, improved in 1809 by English technician John Heathcoat, whose embroidered and laminated knits translated into elegant dresses over a satin background.

Men's attire, 1825-1830

Illustrations in *Costumes Parisiens*, 1816 and 1824

FASHION AND THE INDUSTRIAL REVOLUTION

England's Industrial Revolution (1760-1830) brought with it important innovations in the textile field with the introduction of machinery for cotton spinning powered by human energy (such as the spinning jenny), hydraulics (such as the water-frame), and the invention of the mechanical loom. These developments made mass production possible, and as a result the price of fabric decreased and became affordable for the middle class. Homes and wardrobes became more hygienic thanks to decorative elements and easy- to-wash undergarments. All of the cotton produced in England was acquired through the colonies. Through the cotton business, England, which had a rather important industry, became one of the world centres for prints. Among the novelties in fashion, worth mentioning is the invention of the safety pin in 1849 and the sewing machine in 1851 by Isaac Merrit Singer. In 1849 as well, a chance intuition of Parisian tailor Jolly-Berlin translated into the process of dry cleaning that eliminated stains with turpentine. An Australian named Pullers improved the technique in 1866, opening a cleaning service in the United Kingdom with pick up through the postal service. Goods and services that had been the privilege of the elite now became available to the general public. Everything that had been considered a luxury was considered normal and, beyond that, a necessity. After 1860, the circulation of ready-to-wear clothes filled the markets. In 1862, Charles Butterik created sewing patterns that allowed for making an exact copy of all types of clothing, including all the refinements and smallest details. Around 1870, the first designed undergarments appear. In Europe and America, the big department stores emerged: Bon Marché and Au Printemps in Paris, Selfridge's and Whiteley's in London and Macy's in New York.

Carl Joseph Begas, *The Begas Family*,
1821, Cologne

Charles-Émile-Callande de Champmartin, *Madame de Mirbel*, 1835, Versailles

Charles Boisfremont de Boulanger, *Portrait of Countess Emilia Sommariva Seillere*, 1833, Milan

ROMANTICISM

During the Biedermeier period (1815-1848), an artistic movement defined as a "romantic genre" in vogue among the German and Austrian bourgeoisie, it was not unusual for the wealthy to express difficult concepts in the language of flowers. Every species corresponded to a short sentence and had a conventional meaning that allowed young lovers to express without reservations their feelings to their beloved and initiate a silent correspondence according to the established courtship rules. In the first half of the 19th century, the patriarchal family remained predominant. The period's ideal woman was an obedient and loyal wife, a thoughtful and attentive mother, an angel living placidly at home tending to the household chores and having little interaction with the outside world. With loving hands she beautified towels, linens, tablecloths, pillows, hassocks, stools and chairs, according to the reigning fashion. Floral embroideries were preferred, the beauty and gracefulness of which was increased by the delicacy of the colours, expressing the secret meaning of each flower. While during the Romantic period women were considered fragile creatures in need of protection, the ideal man was a hero that embodied noble and patriotic sentiments. Garments tended to differentiate between the characteristics of the sexes and were expected to be appropriate to location and

circumstances, in accordance with the prevailing standards of elegance at the time. Men's hair was often unkempt, with natural curls and large sideburns that covered the cheeks; around their necks they wore scarves or wide silk cravats. The three-piece suit (trousers, vest and jacket), considered the "modern suit", acquired multiple though minimal variations. The trousers were wide at the top, to emphasize the volume of the pelvis, with stirrups to give them an inclined hang. The restrained suit, made of cloth or corduroy and impeccably cut, had a fitted elegant look. The jacket had a fitted waist with a long tail reaching to the middle of the thigh. It has a long shawl collar with moderately wide lapels that surround the shoulders. The coat was fitted as well, redingote-style, with low joined mutton sleeves. The frivolity of a damask or velvet vest was accepted, lending a bit of colour. The cylindrical hat was used every day while the bicorne was reserved for court affairs. Shoes tended to be flat, made of black leather, with a tapered shape, normal heels and sometimes with a buckle. Women's fashion was inspired by medieval Gothic style and the Renaissance, emitting an air of historical recreation.

Franz Xaver Winterhalter, *The Duke of Wellington with Sir Robert Peel*, 1844

Franz Xaver Winterhalter, *Portrait of Helene Mecklenburg-Strelitz*, 1839

Moritz von Schwind, *In the Artist's House*, 1860, Munich

Left: Franz Xaver Winterhalter, *Maria Luisa of Belgium*, 1841

Fashion embraced pastel hues. The waist was fitted with bodices of French manufacture and the skirt became longer, enhanced and enlarged with ample creases, leaving the feet exposed. The girth needed to be as close as possible to the 40 cm (16 inches) ideal, something achieved by squeezing the body with all sorts of devices. The bust was supported with fan-shaped whalebone or steel boning, covered with fabric and involved complicated locking systems with embroidered buttonholes through which ribbons were threaded (they were later substituted with metallic buttonholes and hooks). Drawings from the period depict amusing morning scenes where the husband attempts to fasten his wife's corset, thereby ensuring his total control of her sexual life. In 1823, a mechanical corset was introduced with pulleys and minuscule mechanisms on the back that made the article resemble an orthopaedic restraint corset rather than a woman's fashion accessory, though they did facilitate quick and independent fastening. Heart-shaped or bateau plunging necklines shaped the naked shoulders. Reinforced petticoats, stuffed and overlapped to provide volume to the lower part, held the dresses in place. This lower part was in contrast to small, playful hairstyles with bent braids set with hairspray or little buns fastened with pins and curls on the sides. These Chinese or giraffe-style hairdos elongated the neck and were considered appropriate for attending

TREATISE ON ELEGANT LIVING

In 1830, in France, author Honore de Balzac (1799-1850) published *Treatise on Elegant Living*, which states that "attire is the expression of society" and, therefore, it reflects in all of its forms moral attitudes and ideological choices. Balzac divides humankind into three classes that represent three existential styles distinguishable by their attire and by their use of the carriage, the means of transport in vogue at the time. The "instrument man" is a working man who, though lacking individuality, is comfortable with the steam engine, wears "leather trousers, two fathoms of blue cloth and shoes". In this category Balzac also includes the "less degraded types of working life" who tend to lead a vulgar existence, "misuse artificial collars" and aspire to a "little coat and gloves made of coarse linen for their wives". Ascending the social ladder, we find the thinking man, who "makes his own revolution under dignified embroidered dress coats" while remaining a slave to his own professional obligations. These are middle class doctors, lawyers, artisans, bureaucrats and businessmen for whom "luxury is a means to save" and whose "wives wear necklaces and earrings". To these we must add the parvenues, the nouveaux riches, who boast of their bought noble titles and their servants dressed in livery (in order to lead an elegant life, having a servant was a must)

and their reserved boxes at the theatre. Lastly, there is the category of the idle man, devoted to rest, the only one that can be considered fashionable and that thoroughly enjoys what he owns. It would be an error, however, to think that being rich is sufficient to aspire to an elegant life because, to the contrary: "Everything that wealth reveals is inelegant", since wealth is simply a means and "can neither be seen nor felt". Critical of the elegance of the bourgeoisie, immersed in a "society where differences have disappeared",

Balzac states that true elegance is an attitude, an instinctive skill that is identified, above all, with the art of savoir vivre, "the science of manners". The only exception is the artist: "His leisure is his work, his work is his rest, and elegant or dishevelled, he may choose to wear the shirt of a peasant or the tail coat of a fashionable man. He does not abide by the rules: he dictates them." Thus, it must be made clear that "the luxury of simplicity is not the simplicity of luxury", because dressing is "science, art, habit and feeling".

balls. They wore minuscule shoes tied with satin laces. Little hats with visors and wide brims framed the face, always shaded under parasols and umbrellas, as paleness was considered a sign of distinction and suntans were for peasants and country women who did not follow the dictates of fashion and dressed modestly, especially on working days. During the first part of the 19th century, the characteristics specific to the regional dress of rural areas throughout Europe, often accompanied with whimsical hairstyles, began to take root. Young and daring women such as Princess Sissi, married in Vienna to Emperor Joseph I of Austria, cemented their reputation as elegant horsewomen, wearing a long skirt down to the ground, a fitted, short jacket and a small cylindrical hat enhanced with a veil. Wedding dresses adapted to their symbolic meaning: surrounded by pomp and splendour they were representative not only of an extraordinary event but also of the condition of dependence of women. A little later, the crinoline and the wasp waist –achieved with the skilled use of stays, which kept the bust erect and parted the breasts, not without serious health consequences– became the norm. Women continued sacrificing comfort for the sake of appearances. Around 1840, women's dresses evoked Rococo repetition. The stiff corset had a pointy shape, skirts were longer and wider and of various colours, overlapping with an excess of pleats and ribbons used in the bodice and the sleeves as well. Held together in layers of petticoats, skirts were embellished with bows, lace and frills that reflected the tastes of 19th century ladies. In order to reduce the waist, the corset "a la paresseuse", or "lazy corset", with elastic lacing that allowed women to put it on without the help of a maid, was used.

Franz Xaver Winterhalter, *Portrait of Countess Varvara Alekseyevna Musina-Pushkina*, around 1855, Saint Petersburg

Franz Xaver Winterhalter, *The Empress Eugénie surrounded by her Ladies in Waiting*, 1855, Castle of Compiegne, France

CRINOLINE

Crinoline is a hoop skirt made with a stiff material and supported with a filling consisting of the mane of a horse (hence its French name, as "crin" means "horse hair"), or straw. Worn on top of the corset, it was bell-shaped, tied at the waist and helped provide structure to women's dresses. The volume it offered in the lower part made it difficult to move, which, in turn, forced women to adopt more feminine and graceful movements. Designer Frederick

Worth transformed crinoline into a cage-shaped structure, a sort of armour made of increasingly wider circles that disproportionately inflated the skirt. The width of the dress was an appealing characteristic because it put a certain distance between the feminine figure and the surrounding space, thus avoiding overly close contact between the sexes, something that might have upset the bourgeois mores of the period. The materials used ranged from iron stays to wicker, baleen or steel sheets, all lined with fabric. Upper class women and others used them to imitate Eugenie, the wife of Napoleon III, considered a style icon who once attended a court dance wearing a white dress embellished with more than one hundred tulle frills. It appears that there was a competition between the French empress and the queen of England as to who was the most elegant. The challenge involved the range of the skirt, which, in 1865, had a radius of 7 meters. In order to alleviate the innumerable discomforts that such a wide shape and stiffness caused, Worth soon substituted the crinoline with the "semi-crinoline", one that was asymmetrical, flat at the front and puffy at the back, granting the figure a characteristic triangular curve when seen from the side. Supported in this fashion, dresses were covered with stripes and layers of frills, trimmings and elegant drapes, indicating a woman's status.

Costumes Parisiens, 1830

THE SECOND EMPIRE
OR VICTORIAN PERIOD

The role of women was affected by the political transformations that shook Europe in 1848, the result of the many revolts undertaken by the bourgeoisie that revolutionized the idiosyncrasy of the period and influenced customs and attitudes. After the abdication of Louis Phillipe, the adversary of the working class and the representatives of the petit bourgeoisie, the Second Republic was proclaimed. However, in 1851 a coup d'etat placed the executive power in the hands of Napoleon III, architect of the Second Empire (1851-1870). Thanks to the guarantees of social order that the new regime provided to the ascending capitalism, France experienced in those years extraordinary development under the slogan "Enrichissez-vous!" ("Get rich!") launched by François Guizot, a French politician and historian. To raise the level of society, Guizot believed more in merit than in fortune and more in work than in inheritance, placing more faith in the benefits of education than in the advantages of speculation. Immense fortunes were amassed in a period of time while the country converted to the religion of saving and making a profit. In the second half of the 19th century, fashion became more rational. Simple domestic garments such as the *matinée* (loose dress for walking around the house in the morning) or the *deshabille robe* (worn in the morning) gained distinction. Also popular were clothes designed for strolling along promenades. More elaborate, these garments were worn in the afternoon. An example of one is the *princesse*, a one-piece dress that appeared around 1865 and was an immediate success.

James Tissot, *Portrait of a Girl*, 1864, Paris

Franz Xaver Winterhalter, *Countess Alexander Nokolaevitch*, 1859, New York

Next page:
Franz Xaver Winterhalter, *Empress Eugenia dressed as Marie Antoinette*, 1854, New York

From Court Dress to 19th Century Bourgeois Fashion

More luxurious garments were worn in the evening. The volume of hairstyles diminished in the upper part. Hair was black with a part in the middle that divided the two sections, gathered at the nape of the neck and fluffed out at the ears, with prosthetic filling. The custom of paying a visit on a set day to discuss artistic, literary and patriotic matters became widespread among aristocratic men. Starting in the Second Empire, when *soft* furniture was adopted, the drawing room became the typical environment where visitors were entertained, and pieces of tapestry were more highly prized than furniture. Small S-shaped divans with two or three seats, called *confidente* and *indiscreto*, were also regarded highly.

Padding and cushions assumed the colours of the heavy drapes that were an essential element in completing a decorative ensemble. The most common decorative fabrics were brocade, lampasa, monochromatic damask, Chinese satin and hand-embroidered tapestries. There were many similarities between the forms of garments and the decorative elements in the home, the epicentre of social life: the daily dress was adorned with abundant passementerie, the preference of Empress Eugenia, who wanted to show her favour to Lyon manufacturers of this type of trimming or edging. Echoes from the drawing rooms of Countess Clara Maffei or the exquisitely elegant Countess Castiglioni contributed to consolidating a new image of the worldly woman: dynamic,

BERLIN EMBROIDERY

Embroidery of images was one of the preferred occupations of 19th century bourgeois women. The so-called Berlin embroidery, conceived of by a Berlin engravings vendor who, in 1810, produced a series of colour floral designs taken from famous paintings, was one of the most popular types. The designs were sold in packets of twenty and were embroidered on cloth with Berlin wool, the best on the market at the time, with superb results. The designs spread on a massive scale, and the embroideries had a huge repertoire that ultimately included 14,000 motifs, which were developed through repetition and simplification of subject matter coupled with ingenuity and poetry to communicate symbolic meaning. Around 1850, English ladies who embroidered with needles on a frame preferred this technique to produce a wide range of objects: cushions, chair backrests, galleries for drapes, screens, chimney mats, entire hexagonal rugs with flower bouquets, corollas, water lilies, passion flowers and small animals, whose bright colours were highlighted against a black background. Superfluous accessories such as pouches, muffs, slippers, boxes, linings and vanity cases were adorned with borders and edges with embroidered floral bouquets or corollas, substituting Berlin wool with zephyr wool and glass beads from Venice and Bohemia.

Above: Franz Dvorak, *Bedrich Smetana and His Friends*, 1865, Vienna

Boldini, *Verdi in a Top Hat*, 1886, Rome

sophisticated and socially entrepreneurial. Their example awoke in middle class women a desire for more independence, one obtained not without harsh sacrifices.

In 1851, the first World Fair was held in London. During the event, the Crystal Palace was built, which attracted a large number of visitors interested in learning about the numerous innovations in industrial progress. Suddenly, the world seemed smaller; people were travelling and moving more frequently and cultural and economic exchanges between countries increased. In subsequent years, the business Bon Marché opened in Paris followed by the large warehouse of the Louvre in 1855 and the town hall bazaar in 1856. During the 1885 Paris World Fair, sewing machines generated a great deal of interest. While arousing considerable suspicion before the international fair, their popularity soon began to grow thanks to the Singer model (1850) patented in the United States. The discovery of aniline, used to obtain violet, magenta and black dyes, in 1856, inaugurated the era of chemical dyes. In Paris, Charles-Frédéric Worth, considered the founder of haute couture, opened *Maison* on the Rue de la Paix and, in 1864, became the official supplier of Empress Eugenia, while Caroline Reboux was the official stylist of the court. A thin waist remained a categorical imperative while at this time crinoline reached the pinnacle of its width: it was said that the lover of writer Charles Dickens, the actress Nelly Ternan, hid her favourite dog inside it when travelling by train.

Left: Franz Xaver Winterhalter, *Elisabeth of Austria in Dancing Dress*, Vienna, 1865

Around 1860, along with the many stuffed flannel petticoats, starched linen petticoats and short muslin skirts with flounces and long undergarments with lace borders acquired importance. Sleeves adopted the *pagoda* shape, widening at the elbow and leaving visible the lower adorned sleeve as well as the collar with lace flounces. Scarves with heavy silk fringes, large black lace shawls that covered the breasts and crinoline completely, circular capes called *rotonde* or long open jackets and dress coats adorned with decorative fastenings like on knickerbockers were worn over the dress. Worth also introduced the tailor's signature as a distinctive sign of an exclusive fashion garment. To gain public approval, he hit upon an ingenious system. He would have "doubles", chosen for their likeness to potential buyers, model the garments for his customers.

Les petites filles modèles thus were born. The first fashion models in history, they took their first steps among the lights and shadows of the city of lights, among aristocrats and poets, businessmen, bankers, artists' models, artists and painters. In England, the long-lasting reign of Queen Victoria (1837-1901) ensured political stability and economic growth through reforms from which the middle class, devoted to the commercial and colonial expansion of the nation, benefitted the most. Still, at the same time, significant social problems began to emerge. One of the favourite motifs of the Victorian Era is the rose, a universal symbol of beauty. Stems of violets, flowers of the lily with poppies and stalks of wheat, scattered rosebuds and baskets filled with flowers and fruit held in place with a love knot was a nod to childhood, reflecting a middle class style of life attentive to small, tender things. Large brooches (pins) inserted in massive gold and smooth gem mounts, faceted or cut in cabochon, appeared. In 1865 earrings became fashionable again. Black velvet ribbons worn around the neck with a small cameo or hanging gem with the initials of the name of the person wearing it and the name of their beloved were popular. Prominent in the ample necklines were pearl necklaces with few loops, along with bracelets and varied brooches. Always present was the lace or painted fan, with gold or silver sequins and marble, mother-of-pearl or ebony frames, adorned with hard stones or diamonds. The form of men's clothing and accessories was adapted to new functions. The paletot, a straight, comfortable, almost uniform coat or jacket, derived from a three-quarter coat worn by Spanish peasants and worn with straight pants with stripes and squares, appeared. It was worn primarily on trips and during visits to the country, where jackets with velvet collars and overcoats adorned with decorative fastenings along with tall riding boots were also considered elegant.

Later, with some modifications, women also adopted the paleton. In the city, the closefitting frock coat, tube pants with belt loops and fancy vests remained popular. Coinciding with the arrival of the crinoline, men began wearing monochrome outfits, corresponding to the notion of the classic men's suit. For the evening, shirts with breast pieces, cuffs, high starched collars and bowties, metal monocles and the essential cylindrical black top hat became fashionable. Since 1848, the beaver top hat had given way to ones made of varnished cardboard and covered with silk felt.

Years earlier, a folding model that was less cumbersome when it was not being worn had been patented. The period also saw a great flourishing of music. The lyrical operas of Donizetti, Rossini and Verdi, who, in 1853, composed *La Traviata*, as well as arias by

Karl Briullov, *Portrait of Yulia Samoylova with Giovannina Pacini and black boy*, circa 1842

Les Petites Filles modèles

Michele Gordigiani, *Condesa Castiglione*, 1862

Anonymous, *Queen Victoria and her cousin*, 1852

Beethoven, Schubert, Mendelssohn and pieces by Listz and Chopin, became widespread. With the invention of photography, which completely revolutionised the figurative arts by allowing for the immediate and true reproduction of reality, painting developed new expressive languages that aspired to capture the most fleeting and momentary impressions: thus the Impressionist movement was born. While still the province of the elite, a larger number of people became increasingly more interested in fashion, which turned to the press, to the commentaries of urban chroniclers of trends to spread its message. In 1860, the magazine *Mode illustrée, Journal de la famille* was founded. While the spread of the sewing machine accelerated the production process, in 1861 the department store *du Printemps*, followed in 1866 by *Magazzini Riuniti* and in 1869 *La Samaritaine*, appeared in Paris. Emile Zola, in the novel *The Ladies' Paradise*, written in 1883, provides an accurate description of the contagious euphoria that emanated from the merchandise displayed in these establishments.

FINAL DECADES OF THE 19TH CENTURY

At the end of the 19th century democratic ideals called for the elimination of the signs of social difference and men's clothing became increasingly more serious. The black suit consisting of three pieces of the same fabric was commonly worn, confirming the preference for a single colour in the entire garment. The short, straight line was the most popular, which became looser and more comfortable on the whole. The *sack-like* jacket, with straight buttons and barely covering the buttocks, was adopted. The custom of fastening only the first two buttons spread. The tightfitting Dorsay jacket, with slightly fitted selvedge, as well as the "hunting" jacket, a favourite of Victor Emmanuel II, remain popular to this day. Flannel shirts were worn on vacations while in the city, there was a preference for linen shirts with an open-stitched straight collar below the throat. The day-to-day pants were straight and long. The preferred attire of civil servants, managers of factories and professionals consisted of the *finanziera* and top hat, an outfit suited to city life and worn above all by bankers and financiers. The *finanziera* was a long straight knee-length jacket, similar to the redingote, also called *stiffelius* or *prefecticia*, that was worn with a vest, shirt and tie. For evening affairs, the frock coat was de rigeur. Less tightfitting in the waist, in keeping with the trend for comfort, and combined with pants that were narrower in the calves, the frock was reserved for dances, the theatre and elegant meals. The redingote, always crossed and with smaller skirts, possessed the same characteristics. While garments tended to acquire simplicity, the sense of opulence was preserved in accessories. The vest was crossed, and one of its pockets was designed to hold a watch, gold for the wealthy and silver for people of more modest means. The watch was attached to a long chain that hung from the centre and fastened to the buttonhole of the vest with a hook. The most popular ties, at times closed with a pin, were made of satin. In 1890, ties with a knot and two overlapping hanging strands began to appear. The silk bowtie, either dark or with small geometric patterns, was also very popular. Worn with suit jackets, it was occasionally white for evening affairs.

Giovanni Boldini, *Count of Montesquiou*, 1897, Paris

Pierre-Auguste Renoir, *Camille Monet and his son in Argentueil Garden*, 1874, Washington

James Tissot, *The Ball on Shipboard*, 1874,
Londres

Johann Baptist Reiter, *Contemplation in
Negligee*, 1847

From Court Dress to 19th Century Bourgeois Fashion

Édouard Manet, *The Conservatory*, 1878, Berlin

Vittorio Corcos, *Honeymoon*, 1885

Above: Gustave Courbet, *Weaver Asleep*,
1853, Montpellier

Vittorio Corcos, *Governesses in the Country*,
1892, Carpi (Modena)

Right: John Singer Sargent, *Morning Stroll*,
1888

Pierre-Auguste Renoir, *Bal du moulin de la Galette de la galette*, 1876, París

Cylindrical hats and bowler hats with gondola-shape brims were also worn. During this period, the custom of wearing gloves took root. Not quite as essential was the use of canes with ball-shaped handgrips, which were gradually replaced by the black umbrella, which when it was not raining, was carried under the arm with tip pointing backwards. *Pince-nez*-style glasses with oval or round lenses, with metal rims and no side pieces, were worn attached to the jacket lapel with a black cord. The most urbane and sophisticated people used the monocle, embedded in the orbit of the eye. Men were fond of cigars, which, out of politeness, they did not smoke in the presence of women. While male fashion remained basically unchanged, woman's attire became more versatile. In the late 1870s, various skirts were overlapped with flounces at the hems. Initially, stockings and shoes, hidden by crinoline, were not important. Jackets that were narrow in the waist and flared at the sides, with tight-fitting sleeves, jackets with skirts and pleats in the back, were very much in vogue. Hairstyles were not so voluminous, with curls on the neck and little hats with ribbons. Between 1870 and 1875, inflated roundness gave way to the *polisón*, a complement that gathers most of the skirt in the back, creating a circular saddle shape through a series of complex draping effects. The model comes from the hoop skirt or crinoline (in Italian, *faldia*), a stiff cloth petticoat with hoops used to keep the skirt suspended so that it does not hinder walking. To achieve this effect a frame in the shape of a cage or basket, or a cushion positioned at the base of the back, was used. Drapery was more predominant than ever, even in the home, giving rise to the phenomenon of the "interieur

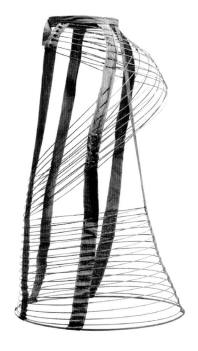

artiste", or interior designer. Consequently, each home contained an unprecedented abundance of objects, works of art and curiosities, making it a small museum. The tendency towards a genuine "ecleticism of style" in all expressive forms was also reflected in clothes: historical references and allusions abounded and there was a clear preferecne for elements taken from the past.

Combined with a tail that reached the ground, the bustle was narrow and subtle in the upper part, tight in the bust and with the neckline closed up to the chin. The lower part, which was very elaborate, provided designers with a opportunity to give expression to their fantasies. They were inspired by the stylistic line popular in the time of Marie Antionette and used different fabrics in large quantities. Around 1876, the volume of skirts moved down and the form of the dress began to accentuate the curve of the sides. Gathered hairstyles became more voluminous with the help of prosthetic braids and buns. Around 1880, women's garments became simpler, acquiring greater sobriety and distinction, though without sacrificing a certain feminine grace, which was also embodied in the *princess* dress, buttoned down the center in the front. At this time, popular French actresses created other lively and whimsical models that gained popularity due to their lavishness. From 1883 to 1889 the bustle, held in place by a *pouf*, a stuffed cushion that formed the characteristic "cul de Paris", became fashionable again. Corsets were increasingly tight, pushing up the breasts, which were covered with adornments, breastpieces and lace ties arranged on the blouse. Jackets adopted a masculine cut and were complemented by capes and leather sleeves. Caricatures from the period compare

James Tissot, *Fashionable Woman* 1883-1885

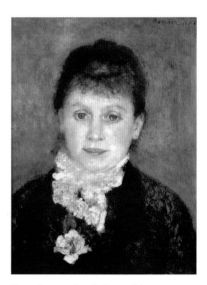

Pierre-Auguste Renoir, *Young Woman with a Veil and Woman with White Scarf,* 1880, Paris

Decorated fabrics by William Morris

Illustration of *The Delineator*, 1898

women to "busty little birds incubating". In the 1890s the bustle was replaced by a corset with a soft petticoat. Fashion imposed a flared skirt that reached down to the calves and was open in the lower part, balanced above by long inflated *gigot*, or leg-of-mutton, sleeves. All women's clothing took on new connotations due to the necessity of responding to more rational, practical and functional criteria. A transformation in attire and daily life occured, and increased attention was paid to standards of hygiene and sports. A new culture of the body emerged that would change the parameters of the figure. More discreet and sober dresses were adopted for daily use while dresses made of more elegant and ostentatious materials were worn for soirees. Elegant capes of Dalmatian velvet, with side openings for the arms, adorned with gold passementerie and fringes made of hair were worn to elegant balls. Capes consisted of three overlapping pieces of increasing length, with a wide square camisole; occasionally the lower border featured a fantastical cut, with several stitches, passementerie embroidery, jet stones and feathers. In summer, a lace cape called a *rotonde* was used. In 1890, the first experiments with nitrocellulose-based artificial silk were conducted.

Some artists embarked on the creation of a new "wardrobe aesthetic", and as a result the atmosphere of innovation that was already prevalent in the visual arts descended upon the field of fashion. William Morris embodied the figure of the artist-artisan, reimagining traditional decorative techniques and restoring them to

Edward VII, 1894

their former splendour. Certain distinctions between women's and girls' fashion were preserved, the latter tending to be more more modest with less flamboyance in the form of jewels and the use of plain colour and simple, sober adornments. With the enthusiam for vacations and visits to spas, which attracted a growing public, modest bathing attire with breeches that reached the calves and pleated bodices appeared.

Bathers adopted relaxed attire consisting of a shirt with a sailor's collar, a belt, of black or navy blue or red wool, adorned with anchors and white rope borders. The use of a wide foam or cloth bathrobe spread. The first sports attire, such as wide, flared cyclist pants, cinched at the ankles with a flexible band and with a little skirt on top, and comfortable leisure clothing, appeared and triumphed. Hairstyles tended towards verticality: the mass of hair rose on top of the head and left the back of the neck bare; occasionally hair was left short on the forehead, forming thick bangs. Encouraged by the development of the railway, travel became fashionable. This phenomenon gave rise to a wardrobe consisting of more robust and darker fabrics as well as a series of short or long coats depending on the type of dress. The most popular garment for boys and girls was the sailor's suit. This consisted of a navy blue blouse gathered at the waist, with a large white piqué collar, square in the back and trimmed with straight braids and anchors in the angles, and breeches for boys and pleated skirts for girls. A cap with braids in the winter and a wide-brimmed straw hat with ribbon around the crown in summer were indispensable.

All the nations of Europe embraced the novelties arriving from England and France while contributing variations according to local requirements. In the final decade of the century, the "costume tailleur" took root. This was a three-piece woman's garment created by the English tailor John Redfern, who, in 1881, opened a store in Paris. The *tailleur* was known as the "jacket suit" or "tailor suit" in Spain and *abito alla mascolina* in Italy, in 1888. The name refers to the execution of a precise cut that required the participation of a male tailor (in French, *tailleur*), while the female tailor was called the *couturière* ("seamstress").

Antonio de la Gándara, *Maria Hardouin D'Annunzio*, 1898

Federico Zandomeneghi, *Gril with Flowers*, 1894

20th Century

FASHION IN 1900-1910

Alfons Mucha, Manifesto per le ferrovie del Principato di Monaco, Monaco Monte Carlo, 1990

At the turn of the century, the atmosphere that imbued the Belle Epoque was enthusiastic and optimistic. Demographic growth particularly had an effect in Europe, where jobs in the factories gradually substituted work in the countryside. In opposition to the bourgeois upper class of professionals, merchants and businessmen, the working class emerged. The process of modernization reached the world of fashion as well, with considerable progress in the use of the first synthetic dyes for fabrics that were more resistant to washing. The wool and cotton industries experimented a great surge, while rayon was first marketed in Britain, in 1905. Meanwhile, women struggled for emancipation through education and commitment to social causes.

The suffragettes defended total legal equality and began their fight for the right to vote. In 1908, a group of textile workers in New York City died in a fire on 8 March inside factory 152 while protesting their despicable working conditions. In their honour, International Women's Day is now celebrated. In the final days of the 19th century, Art Nouveau was the major trend. Inspired by Japanese art, it tends to blur the boundaries between crafts and fine art. Artists became interested in the relationship between drawing and project in the applied arts, the execution techniques of which became more painstaking. This represented the birth of design, where the aesthetic quality of every object is not at odds with its usefulness. Sinuous lines, plain backgrounds and stylized plant embellishments predominated in fabrics, embroideries, jewellery, posters and illustrations by Alphonse Mucha. Photography became a vehicle for the transmission of fashion, clothing and their characteristic expressions.

The Exposition Universelle, Paris' world fair held in 1900, included a Pavillon de l'Élégance with French haute couture creations alongside more traditional ones. The shapes of the garments reinterpreted previous models with less volume and more flow. Women's silhouette gradually changed, shifting from the S-line,

Suffragettes protesting in the early 20th century

typical of the change from one century to the next, to the Empire line that was introduced around 1910. Dresses could be one piece or two-piece with the bodice and skirt made of the same fabric.

The thin waist, marked by the corset, highlighted the bell-shaped skirt with a rounded tail. For strolls, the suit gained prominence. The skirt was at an angle, and the outfit had a matching jacket with shapely, open flaps over a busy feminine blouse. Ivory, wisteria, peach and cornflower were the preferred tones for the blouse, made of silk muslin or wool, fastened at the back with little buttons and embellished with a cravat, jabot, camisole and cuffs, guipure lace, embroideries or lace placket. Embellishments were interchangeable and were ordered via mail order catalogue. Fashion's influence also reached lingerie: nightgowns, undergarments and dresses for aristocratic women and the demimondaines. Curved cuts for jackets and bolero jackets, collars embellished with soutache, coats and capes with crystal, mother-of-pearl and enamel buttons were common. Short-leg boots or kidskin shoes with carrete heels were the footwear of choice.

Etiquette conditioned the choice of dresses and regulated rituals at receptions and on strolls. Private occasions or social gatherings marked the tempo of everyday life, determining day or afternoon attire, the mattinée for the home and a cape for visitors. It was difficult to change without help from maids. Even less well-to-do women wore hats, an indispensable accessory. More practical attire was adopted for sports activities, which were increasingly appreciated by women: tennis, archery, skating, fishing, horseback riding and golf. Skirts now reached the ankle, facilitating movement.

Early 20th century suit

Keren Ben-Horn, 1900-1903

Left: Ulisse Caputo, Lavoro di sera, 1909

Gloves came in contrasting colours while parasols used for strolls had sculpted handles.

The wealthy classes attended the theatre, opera and concerts and frequented parlours, exclusive circles and charity galas. Highly decorated ball gowns displayed an exaggerated taste in the choice of ornaments and fabrics. Petticoats were lighter, more transparent and made of embroidered tulle. Meshes over satin and ribbons over organza extended throughout the entire dress. Luxeuil lace and velvet flowers embellished the shoulders or neckline, high-

Henri Gervex, *Five Hours at Paquin's*, 1906

GUSTAV KLIMT AND THE WIENER WERKSTÄTTE

The son of a goldsmith from Bohemia, Gustav Klimt was the driving force of Secession in Vienna (Austria's answer to Art Nouveau), a group committed to the definition of the total work of art. His paintings express a languid sensuality, enveloped in beauty, among geometric elements and frames embellished with gold leaves, the product of the artist's familiarity with this metal. Klimt had a relationship with Emilie Flöge (1874-1952), designer of the reform dress who, in 1904, opened with her sister Schwestern Flöge one of the most important couture shops of Vienna's avant-garde. Eighty seamstresses and three master cutters worked in the shop. Embraced as a means of liberating women from their dependency on French tastes, the fluid reform dresses pleased Austrian feminists. Klimt collaborated with Emilie on a series of sack dresses that both of them wore. He also collaborated with the Wiener Werkstatte (Vienna's Workshops), a famous production community linked to the world of design and founded in 1903 by Josef Hoffmann (1870-1956) and Kolo Moser (1868-1918). The association produced decorative objects and utensils for domestic use and also had a section devoted to jewellery. It was very important on the European applied arts scene, to the point where Paul Poiret paid a visit to it in 1911.

The Delineator, 1901

Paul Cesar Helleu, *Portrait of a Woman*, 1909

Left: *Illustration in Les Modes*, 1903

THE MILLINER

This profession, which emerged in the 19th century, provided working-class women with a privileged job that offered creative uniqueness. Wearing an exclusive hat communicated social well-being. Milliners' shops were crowded with ladies who went to admire the latest novelties, exhibited on wooden supports, and came and went choosing the model appropriate for their faces, according to the latest styles. The hats sat on top of large hairdos achieved with the addition of hairpieces and fillings held in place with large ornamental hairpins. Among the first hats in fashion were the rice straw *Labbè*, the colourful *Yedda* with erect strips similar to a cornucopia of flowers and muslin and velvet ornaments, or the refined Louis XV tricorne with large buckles adorned with gemstones, ribbons and feathers. Hats were worn as well in the theatre and game rooms. In Paris, in 1910, the work of milliners reached high levels of quality. In fact, one could order unique pieces from Georgette or Caroline Reboux, who created hats for the actress Réjane. Once finished, the hat was wrapped in paper, put in a hatbox and sent directly to the customer's home via the *trottines*, or younger employees.

Georges Lemmen, *La modista*, 1901

INTIMATE APPAREL

In Milan, the editor Ulrico Hoepli published the *Giornalle illustrato della Biancheria* for women, men, children and the home. Around 1906, nightgowns, negligées, underskirts, the double corset-petticoat in silk crepe or duchesse satin, intimate garments with pleated frills, fitted bodices and day and night shirts all followed the Empire style. Stockings were embellished with patterns of small monograms and rims with Liberty-style shapes. Women's wardrobes included several types of clothing, and the shape of the corset also had to be altered, evolving toward models that reached the waist with closefitting tow-coloured intersecting ribbons and longer ribbons that enveloped the hips. Among the fabrics used were knitted materials and slightly elastic and breathable mesh recommended for sports. In 1914, the American Carezza Crosby patented the first model for a bra, though it met with little success.

lighting long pearl necklaces. Princess Alexandra was responsible for the introduction of the *collier de chien* fashion (dog collar), an emblem of aristocratic elegance, which she used to hide an ugly scar. Evening gloves were long and enveloping. Night clutches with polychrome beads from Murano or Bohemia with metallic, silk or velvet closings and embroidered with sequins and little chords were ideal cases for keeping dance cards and opera binoculars.

Men's fashion still looked to the Anglo-Saxon model as a reference, inspired by restrained London elegance. King Edward VII owned the largest wardrobe in the world, and his tailor was Henry Poole. Aristocrats and the affluent seeking to prosper socially copied his eclectic, somewhat informal style. Day attire in the city included a pearl-grey bowler hat with a curved brim trimmed with satin.

The cut of the jackets was less stiff and shorter with the buttons kept high on the chest. Younger men wore fedora hats, a loose model of grey felt with a hatband. For more formal occasions, they wore a double-breasted frock coat or morning coat, a jacket with buttons in the middle and parted tails combined with striped trousers and a vest. A top hat, cane and gloves completed the image of the gentleman, who had to adopt restrained movements and gestures.

Princess dress by Redfern, 1906

PARIS AND HAUTE COUTURE

Paris was the paradise of haute couture, and the Rue de la Paix – where C.F. Worth's atelier, managed by tsons Gaston and Jean-Philippe, was located – was one of its most elegant streets. This famous street was also where the shops of Jeanne Paquin, Jacques Doucet and sisters Sylvie and Jeanne Boue, frequented by the wealthiest ladies of high society, who went at least twice a year to Paris to update their wardrobes, were found. Many feminine beauties were immortalized by Giovanni Boldini's brushstrokes and the incisive lines of Cesar Helleu, who illustrated social chronicles in the French magazine Les Modes, read in London, Berlin and New York. Paquin, who in 1906 launched the "Empire" silhouette with Poiret, had a considerable number of people working for him and was the first to open branches in the major capitals, including Buenos Aires and Madrid. Other maisons, founded by Louise Cheruit, Jean Dessès and Georges Doeuillet,

offered fashion articles and accessories. The house Callot Soeur distinguished itself by its profusion of trimmings, ribbons, godets and frills, which were identified with the euphoria of the historical moment. The models were falsified by foreign buyers and copied, in more inexpensive versions, using machine-made lace manufactured in the new textile factories. Product lines were highly varied and affordable for everyone. The latest novelties were exhibited in the shop windows of the main stores: La Belle Jardinière, La Samaritaine, Au Printemps and Les Galeries Lafayette. Au Bon Marché and Le Louvre, which bought wholesale from couturiers, attracted a growing public by offering three categories of products: ready-to-wear articles of clothing, semi-ready clothes and tailored garments. Charles Butterick's catalogue offered patterns for making garments at home, allowing people to be fashionable in an affordable way.

Design by Charles Frederick Worth, around 1900

Jean Paquin, around 1900

For vacations in the country and playing sports, a three-piece garment of rustic tweed or with a chessboard-pattern print in various colours, or, alternatively, a free-form ensemble in contrast to a soft hat of the type preferred by James Joyce, was worn. The Norfolk jacket, designed for hunting, had two symmetrical box pleats on the front and the back as well as a belt. It was combined with short pantaloons and high leggings. The three-piece garment in beige canvas, combined with a canotier with a hatband, or the double-breasted blue blazer with flannel trousers with cuffs, was adequate for the summer. In Paris, renowned jewellers René Lalique and Georges Fouquet sought out original designs and high-quality elaboration.

The actress Sarah Bernhardt made a name for herself playing the roles of Cleopatra and Medea, wearing one of the iconic pieces of the period: a large enamelled gold snake with an opal head that enveloped her wrist three times, becoming a bracelet that was connected to the hand through a ring with a chain. Necklace collections opted for enamel, ivory, horn and hard stones instead of gems, featuring unique pieces with plant shapes alongside languid feminine faces or little dragonflies or butterflies with open wings.

Left: Camille Clifford

Above: Giovanni Boldini, *Walking in the Bois de Boulogne*, Ferrara, 1909

Below left: Summer men's fashion, around 1900

Gibson's girls

Among the most popular images of the period were the "Gibson girls", characters invented by Charles Dana Gibson, an illustrator for *Life Magazine*. Inspired by his wife, Irene Langhorne, he created the prototype of the emancipated woman for American women. While it was a modern idea, the Gibson's girls' beauty included an ideal waist of barely 45 cm, like that of actress Camille Clifford, achieved with corsets that caused serious health problems. Movies, photography and postcards popularized legendary feminine models with a strong temperament, such as the Spanish dancer Agustina Carolina Otero, nicknamed *La Bella Otero*. California dancer Isadora Duncan popularized a free and loose style of dance performed barefoot, far from the academic rigor of classical dance, which harmonized with the natural motions of the body.

Isadora Duncan

FILMS

Nuovomondo, Emanuele Crialese (2006); wardrobe by Mariano Tufano

My Fair Lady, George Cukor (1964); wardrobe by Cecil Beaton and Michael Neuwirth

Portrait of a Lady, Jane Campion (1996); wardrobe by Janet Patterson

FASHION IN THE 1910s

The first quarter of the 20th century was marked by the birth of the avant-garde. German Expressionism, futurism, cubism, constructivism and abstract art were intellectual and artistic movements set out in programmatic manifestoes that experimented with new languages in contrast with current ideas. Art became aware of the creative potential of fashion, recognizing its cultural and social identity. Artists gained experience with garment and fabric designs, drawing scenes and wardrobes for performances, becoming efficient illustrators or comic artists or simply expressing through their work the aesthetic tastes and the disenchanted atmosphere that impregnated the early 20th century. Women still preferred the empire silhouette and opted for a more natural, soft line. By 1902, in Belgium, architect Henry Van de Velde was committed to substantial Reform of feminine attire that favoured functionality, hygiene and simplification. De Velde theorized the principle of "form follows function" in order to make aesthetic style coincide with lifestyle. Experimenting with the notion of "fashion-architecture", he worked with the Reform dress and designed for his wife, Maria Sèthe, several "reception dresses" in which he attempted to free the body from the market's restrictions. His ideas, very advanced for the time, began to spread throughout Europe, where the demand to abolish the enslavement of the corset, which deformed the bone structure and caused fainting fits and internal organ diseases, emerged.

Paul Poiret in France and Mariano Fortuny in Venice directed their creativity toward a more fluid and clean style, one that would better reflect new living conditions. The skirt became tubular and straight, interrupted by a strip of fabric that narrowed the silhouette under the knees and made walking more difficult. The invention of the hobble skirt is attributed to Paul Poiret (1879-1944), who was influenced by Japanese aesthetics and added to it extra European

Vittorio Corcos, *Reading by the Sea*, 1910

THE FASHION OF FUTURISM

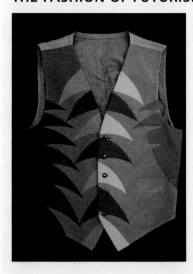

The *Futurist Manifesto* concerning men's fashion was published in 1914 by Giacomo Balla. The Anti-Neutral Clothing experimented with polychrome decorative evolutions over scarfs and women's shawls, vests and accessories. In the name of a new model of functional clothing, the myth of dynamism flooded fashion with new energy, filling it with colours and literally subverting the conventional identity of the bourgeois man. In 1916, Balla experimented with "loud ties". It was a revolutionary, playful and democratic form of fashion where the role of accessories such as modifiers, geometric elements of coloured fabrics for use depending on one's inspiration, was important. In 1920, Vincenzo Fani's (Volt) *Futurist Manifesto of Women's Fashion* was published, proposing the use of unconventional and inexpensive fabrics. In the same year, Marinetti clearly expressed his position in his *Agains Female Luxury manifesto*. In 1933, other artists wrote the *Manifesto of the Italian Necktie* and the *Manifesto of the Italian Hat*. Fortunato Depero published the last one, *The Victory Dress*, in 1942.

Illustration in *Les Modes*, 1902

Enrico Prampolini, 1916

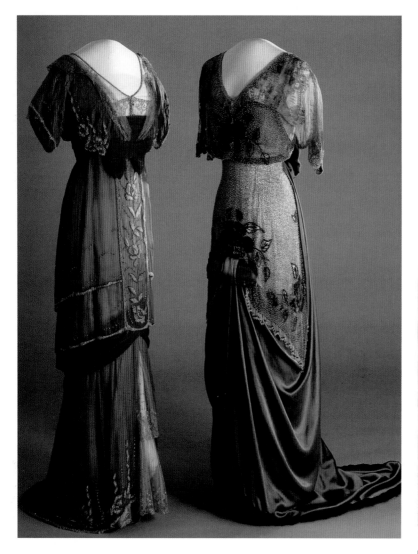

Illustration by George Barbier, 1914

Dresses for Queen Maud of Norway,
1910-1913

suggestions inspired by the kimono and Serge Diaghilev's (1872-1929) ballets russes. Poiret, a visionary son of a fabric merchant, created highly impactful garments that included the Confucious coat (1905), the Lola Montes model (1906), the Josephine dress (1907) and the screen tunic (1913-14), making him the uncontested protagonist of fashion until the onset of World War I. Poiret's unheard-of success was due to the demand for exoticism triggered by the fabulous wardrobe that Leon Bakst (1866-1924) created for *Cleopatra* (1909) and *Scherezade* (1910), which seduced Parisian women into falling in love with small fabric turbans, tiaras with plumes and jewel bands that accompanied asymmetric tunics and loose caftans over sultan skirts or trouser skirts of Turkish harem inspiration. Dance emphasized the visual expressivity of movements, the rhythm of which assumed the cadence of the luminous hues of turning veils and drapes, creating magic-erotic tensions. Poiret was the first designer to realise that if he associated his name with a line of perfumes he would more efficiently connect with women's subconscious, thereby influencing not only the way they dressed but also their way of life. The prototype of the fascinating woman-odalisque was born, a seductive figure in a nightgown and a cape enveloped in a long feather boa. Long finishing elements made of leather and muffs and fur stoles emphasized the idea of daring sensuality.

Girl on a Bicycle

THE DELPHOS GOWN
BY MARIANO FORTUNY

Mariano Fortuny created his first
Delphos gown in 1907, drawing
inspiration from the Charioteer
of Delphi and the soft creases of
classical sculptures. He patented
the prototype in Paris, in 1909,
and continued to develop his
invention in infinite variations
until his death in 1949. The
model consists of a simple satin
tube, made of four or five fabrics
sewn together lengthwise, that
extended upwards and had
openings for the neck and arms.
The Delphos, shaped from within
thanks to strips that defined the
armhole from the underarm to
the shoulder, adapts freely to the
silhouette, subtly revealing it.
The tunic models sometimes had
belts called *kolpos* or braided silk
cords embellished with Murano
beads. The Fortuny design
foresaw superimpositions of
elements that allowed for infinite
variations while using only a few
pieces. He experimented printing
with pigments on velvet, with
superimposed metallic colours to
create shifting reflections.

Marcello Dudovich, 1912.

ICONS OF ELEGANCE:
GABRIELE D'ANNUNZIO

Gabriele D'Annunzio (1863-1938), author of the novel *The Pleasure*, had a close and sincere relationship with fashion. A true style icon, D'Annunzio demonstrated a deep sense of aesthetics that he embraced as an absolute value his entire life, which he conceived as a work of art. This led him to surround himself with rare and precious objects in his home/mausoleum Il Vittoriale in Gardone Riviera and to care for his own wardrobe obsessively, aware that fashion constituted one of the most innovative languages of the period.

Impeccably elegant, he always wore clothes of exquisite manufacture, combining diverse fashions and styles "Made in Italy" or abroad. According to the poet, in fact, "the true value of the article of clothing comes from the tailor; it comes, let us say, from the author's signature". His civilian garments included double-breasted jackets, diplomat suits and dinner jackets made in wool or silk by the most prominent couturiers of the period. As an officer, he wore the uniform of the Cavalry, Assault and Lancers. D'Annunzio scrupulously chose loafers and ankle boots, custom-made in soft

FILMS

Titanic (1997), James Cameron
Chéri (2009), Stephen Frears

The series *Downton Abbey* covers a period of ten years, from 1912 to 1922.
This events of this decade would change the course of history and open the door to a completely renewed society. Fashion, above all women's fashion, changed gradually, with moments of radical upheaval. The dresses seen in *Downton Abbey* cover all the stages of this process.

Giovanni Boldini, *Lady in Pink Dress*, Ferrara, 1916

leather. At home, he wore theatrical silk, velvet or satin smoking jackets. It was said that he had 365 of them and wore a different one every day.

He collected with reverential care all articles of clothing, even underwear, as objects that identified him as a "luxury animal", as he liked to define himself. D'Annunzio, called *il Vate*, embodied an elitist, eccentric and extravagant elegance, eventually becoming the prototype of the modern dandy that creates a cult in his own image via his choice of attire.

He wrote daily as well as lengthy social chronicles where he described the characteristics of clothing, adopting the role of *arbiter elegantiarum* of high society. He gave a new name to the Milanese department store Aux Villes d'Italie, which he re-christened as *La Rinascente*, adding the catchphrase, "L'Italia nova impressa in ogni foggia" (The new Italy in all styles).

FASHION IN THE 1920s

After World War I (1914-1918), the process of women's emancipation seemed irreversible. Women had adopted comfortable and simple attire, similar to that of men, and did not want to relinquish it. In England, the suffragettes' fight culminated in 1918, when they obtained the right to vote for women, which was ratified in the United States as well in 1920. New trends appeared in art, music, movies and fashion. Before long, a strong desire for freedom was in the air; rules of etiquette changed and women began to smoke in public. Entertainment and leisure activities, dances, travel, cruises and vacations became trendy. All of this set the stage for the exuberant atmosphere of the Roaring Twenties, dominated by Hollywood's growing influence, which spread the insouciance of American lifestyle. The most famous actors became role models: Rodolfo Valentino, Clark Gable, Louise Brooks, Clara Bow, Gloria Swanson and Marlene Dietrich.

A CHI LA PIOGGIA . . . . . A NOI..!

Marcello Dudovich, Pirelli advertisement, 1925

Blues, jazz and ragtime, musical genres of African-American origin and popularized by musicians such as Louis Armstrong and Duke Ellington, who wore satin shirts and multi-coloured vests in striking hues, triumphed. In nightclubs in London, Paris, Berlin, New York and Washington, Josephine Baker, the Ebony Venus, performed wearing only little skirts made of feathers or bananas. Dance fever spread quickly everywhere. The public frantically danced the Charleston and tasted the pleasure of living to the foxtrot beat. Skirts became noticeably shorter and after 1924, the use of flesh-toned silk stockings became popular. Dancing gowns revealed the shoulders, had a low-cut neckline and low waist, were straight and ended in asymmetrical silk muslin scallops or were covered with sequin or crystal embroideries and had a layers of

Marlene Dietrich, 1920

fringe that moved to the rhythm of the music. The design flattered the new feminine figure, which was thin and svelte, without curves and moved with androgynous aplomb. Women embraced cute and restrained haircuts *à la Garçonne*, the character in Victor Margueritte's 1922 book, which symbolized freedom and were considered scandalous for the period. Short hair cut like a boy's represented a radical change that allowed for wearing little fitted hats pulled down over the eyes that completely covered the forehead. French stylist François Marcel introduced this haircut with waves. At soirees, little feather crowns that created a kind of halo around the face were a hit. Ostrich, swan and bird of paradise feathers were used for boas, fans and coiffures. Diadems were made of soft fabrics, tulle embellished with jewellery, artificial pearls or diamonds, or, stiff and pointy like tiaras, of golden leather with embroidery or metallic elements. The trendiest purse was the *pochette* made of leather or fabric with Art Deco style inserts or embellishments. Stiff purses made of Persplex or coloured Bakelite, a new material also used in the manufacture of rings, brooches, bracelets and earrings, attracted a great deal of attention. The 1920's were a period of prosperity in America, until the stock market crash of 1929. This wealth allowed the average man to earn enough money from his job to spend on the acquisition of fashionable clothes.

Page from *Delineator*, fashion magazine, 1923

The trends in English fashion continued to influence men's style in the United States. Clothes adopted a slender and tight look, fitting a younger and more athletic figure. Big cities filled with cars experienced a genuine cultural explosion that encouraged initiative and the spirit of adventure. Men's fashion had a sports quality to it, including long trousers with pleats, jacquard sweaters and golf vests for men that travelled in convertibles while wearing the first water-resistant raincoats. The famous pilot Charles Lindbergh set the trend of the leather jacket. American men imitated the style of famous athletes such as football star Red Grange's raccoon coat. Students in Cambridge wore baggy trousers and two-toned shoes. Around 1922, Oxford students launched the extravagant trend of the Oxford bags, extremely loose fitting, cuffed trousers unsuited for work and the object of caricatures. A shirt with a loose collar and low buttons appeared with a regimental tie. The Fair Isle sweater, called jazz a jumper, was a great success.

Due to high demand, the market for quick fashion, a style adopted by all ages, grew. In 1920, British designer Norman Hartnell introduced the utility dress, a linear and inexpensive dress that was adopted during World War II. With a fluid silhouette, a skirt to the knee and ankle strap shoes, this outfit gave women a childish look. America's sweetheart Mary Pickford embodied this ideal with a wide brimmed hat that revealed her ringlets underneath. Jeanne Lanvin proposed similar outfits for mothers and young women in *Gazette du bon ton*.

The influence of Parisian designers such as Patou, Molyneux, Chanel, Lanvin, Lelong and Vionnet was largely felt. Their creations achieved international acclaim thanks to the specialized press and illustrators' designs that contributed to popularizing fashion. Jean

THE CLOCHE HAT

All women wore the most unique headdress of the decade: the cloche. With its simplicity, it equalized duchesses, secretaries, dressmakers and even sophisticated actresses such as Greta Garbo, Anita Page and Marlene Dietrich. The name comes from the French, and its shape is similar to that of a small bell. It is worn like a war helmet, fitted and covering the head completely. Its use led to the prominence of the *Garçonne* haircut. Coco Chanel also wore a felt cloche hat made of one pre-form piece that included the crown and brim. During the 1920's, the cloche hat experimented an evolution and adapted to changes in clothing. At the beginning of the decade, the crown was round and the brim, worn down, up on the forehead or on both sides, was wider. In 1923, the youthful cap, comfortable and easy to wear on a trip or a stroll, became popular. Between 1925 and 1927, the crown became smaller and more fitted, the brim was extremely small and the materials varied.

Patou devoted himself to sports attire, designing long pleated skirts for the famous tennis player Suzanne Lenglen. In 1926, Jeanne Lanvin launched the *robe de style*, which merged the simplicity of modernism with traditional tailoring.

The role of women as directors of several fashion houses emerged. Coco Chanel launched the jersey three-piece tailor-made suit, including a short, straight skirt, sweater and cardigan. The jersey fabrics were embellished with costume jewellery: gold chains and fanciful jewellery made of coloured crystals. Chanel was one of the first women to wear wide and practical slacks, which she appropriated from the men's wardrobe. In 1926, she launched the "petit noir", the little black dress, a short restrained dress of China crepe and illuminated with pearls. The garment, which *Vogue America* called the "Chanel-Ford", an analogy to the T-model American automobile, would become a timeless classic. Coco Chanel did not frown upon suntans, and thanks to her, bronze skin became trendy. She also launched the famous Chanel No. 5 perfume, linking it to her clothing line. Madeleine Vionnet designed bias cut garments that exalted movement. She assembled fabric panels of different shapes, taking advantage of the hang of the fabric and its natural elasticity, and sewed them together, making the pieces glide and granting the dress an asymmetrical appearance. She designed directly over a mannequin of reduced size and later would work on the model's body. Eschewing superfluous embellishments, she preferred solid colours.

ART AND FASHION

In 1919, the Bauhaus, a state technical and art school considered the cradle of contemporary design, was born. The alliance between art, craft and industry was determined to release individual creative potential to the fullest through lectures and seminars and by working in workshops and factories. Functioning until 1933, the school influenced artists and designers all over the world. Among the most significant artistic experiments of the period was the Russian avant-garde. The exponents of Constructivism proposed creating art that appealed directly to the masses and would serve as a source of social progress. They viewed fashion in functional terms and used techniques and materials derived from industrial development. Vladimir Tatlin designed a modular coat consisting of interchangeable parts. Designers Varvara Stepanova and Liubov Popova distinguished garments according to their use. Nadezhda Lamanova created a type of garment that resurrected the traditional Russian dress. According to their theory, the nature of the material should determine the purpose of the article of clothing while form should condition the adornments. Alexandra Exter eliminated even the pattern, designing functional clothing as if they were sculptures and theatrical attire conceived as "body masks". At the Exposition Internationale des Arts Décoratifs, in 1925, the simultaneous fabrics designed by Ukrainian designer Sonia Terk Delaunay, who made her debut in fashion with a patchwork of abstract motifs of her son Charles, were present.

Sonia Delaunay, 1920s

Illustration by Marcello Dudovich, 1925

ICONS OF BEAUTY: FLAPPER GIRLS

In 1921, the first Miss America was elected, and quickly thereafter beauty contests spread. The pages of *Vogue* offered advice on how to apply the perfect makeup with rouge and lipstick. The legendary Louise Brooks embodied the period's female prototype, the flapper girl, flapping being the visible effect of women's liberation. The truly fashionable girl of the 1920's adopted nonconformist attitudes, listened to jazz, danced the Charleston, frequented nightclubs, smoked with a mouthpiece and conversed with grace and ease. Brooks wore short, sliding dresses structured with shoulder pads that showed the legs, long pearl necklaces and feather accessories. She was fond of comfortable shoes, the classic ankle strap or t-strap Mary Janes, perfect for dancing frantically. The twenties' hairdo was a bob, which was straight and parted in the middle with straight bangs. Her eyebrows were groomed and the nape of the neck was left visible while two locks extended toward the cheeks. Her hairdo gave her an innocent yet simultaneously sensual look. In a short period of time, Louise Brooks, who played the role of Lulu in the movie *Pandora's Box* (1929) by Georg Wilhelm Pabst, popularized this boyish cut, also called the shingle bob, coconut bob, Eton crop or Charleston cut, the most demanded women's hairstyle at the time. Francis Scott Fitzgerald described the transformation of the flapper girls in a story called "Bernice Bobs Her Hair".

Ladies' Home Journal, November 1928

Illustration by L. Riccio en Lidel, 1927

Left: Louise Brooks

FASHION ILLUSTRATORS

Illustration by George Barbier

The fashion revolution was made possible above all thanks to the contribution of specialized magazines. Along with the already mentioned American magazines *Harper's Bazaar* (1867) and *Vogue* (1892), the *Gazette du Bon Ton* (1912-1925) and *Art, Goût, Beautè* (1920-1933) appeared. At a time when fashion photography was still in its beginnings, these magazines published designs illustrated by the best artists on a monthly basis, advertising the latest creations of dressmakers (Patou, Poiret, Doucet, Redfern, Worth, Lanvin, Molyneux, etc.). As a result, George Barbier's stylized "template" illustrations were born. He published five volumes of *Ruffles and Frills: Almanach of Style, Present, Past, and Future*, between 1922 and 1925. Erte's extravagant and refined women also took shape. Erte was an astounding designer devoted to the creation of stages and wardrobe for plays, movies, revues and ballets. In 1911, George Lepape illustrated *Les Choses de Paul Poiret*, a catalogue requested by his designer friend. He collaborated with *La Gazette du Bon Ton* and other important fashion magazines, and designed fabrics and advertisement posters as well. Between 1918 and 1938, the number of magazines devoted to women's handwork increased, as more importance was given to "homemade" articles of clothing. The same occurred with sewing machines or knitting machines, which were advertised in major newspapers aimed at the general public.

FILMS

The Kid (1921), by Charlie Chaplin

Flesh and the Devil (1926), by Clarence Brown, with Greta Garbo

Pandora's Box (1928), by Georg Wilhelm Pabst, with Louise Brooks

The Great Gatsby, based on F. Scott Fitzgerald's novel, set in 1922 between Long Island's North Shore and New York City

Downton Abbey, famous English television series

Portada de *Vogue* de Georges Lepape, 1927

FASHION IN THE 1930s

On 29 October 1929, the New Stock Exchange crashed, dragging down with it the economies of all industrialized countries. An unprecedented world economic and financial crisis began, leading to millions of unemployed and what came to be known as the Great Depression. Drastic protectionist measures heavily taxed the export of luxury products to the United States. Work at the French haute couture houses was greatly reduced. Paris was able to maintain its leadership in the international markets thanks to precise strategies of product diversification. Lucien Lelong took as a reference the American industry of serially manufactured clothing,

Future fashions, 1930

drawing from it for his collection *Les robes d'édition*, a 1934 line that preceded the birth of *prêt-à-porter*. At the same time, Chanel kept her exorbitant prices, focusing on a reduced elite, unperturbed by the fact that her linear and modern designs were being copied in innumerable cheap versions.

Other women of great charisma secured their spots in fashion. One was Elsa Schiaparelli, an eclectic and extravagant person who interacted with surrealist intellectuals and artists. Another was the more traditional Madame Gres, who enveloped the bodies of her contemporaries in linear purity, as if they were snow-white columns. English and American designers began to break away from Parisian tastes and developed their own creative gold mine, one more oriented toward the production of classic and casual sport garments. The zipper began to be used. The metallic fastener had already been seen on leather articles and suitcases; in 1923 it appeared on rubber rain boots, also called zipper boots. Lightning zippers were used on children's clothes. Elsa Schiaparelli first applied them to sports clothing for the beach. Later, as a provocation, she used zippers on her jackets and afternoon clothing without concealing them under the fabric. In 1937, the lightning zipper, considered an "innovative idea in tailoring", was introduced in men's trousers. The relationship between fashion and movies became closer and more

ELSA SCHIAPARELLI

An emerging figure of 1930s fashion, the extravagant, cultured and fascinating Elsa Schiaparelli started her career in Paris, supported by Paul Poiret. She was Chanel's main rival and one of the first dressmakers to develop collections around a single theme within the art-fashion coupling. A true pioneer of artistic experimentation, she was influenced by surrealist theories as well as the paintings of Salvador Dalí and Pablo Picasso, employing new materials such as escorce d'arbre (tree bark), tweed and exhibiting a preference for artificial fibres. Endowed with a vibrant imagination, she designed capricious hats such as the inkbottle or upside down shoe, suitable for elegant and open-minded customers. She introduced oneiric references, such as mirrors, elephants, circus people, musical notes, zodiac signs, drawers, lobsters, giant mouths and newspaper pages. She conceived of fashion as, above all, an eternal diversion, one that allowed her to give funny shapes even to the buttons designed for her by Jean Clément: oranges, lemons, eggplants, coffee grains, ballet dancers, lollipops, foals, little bells, corks and dollars.

In addition to her immediate success, some of her ideas survived, such as the accented waist and the use of shoulder pads, the tattoo-jersey, in black and white optical style, with big trompe-l'oeil bows, and the "X-ray pullover", which reproduced a radiography of the human skeleton. In 1935, she moved her Parisian atelier to Place Vendome, where she inaugurated prêt-à-porter, ready-to-sell clothes and objects in standard sizes that were serially produced. Her favourite colour was shocking pink, a chromatic tone that would also lend its name to the perfume and auto-biography of this Italian designer: Shocking Life.

Afternoon dresses, *McCall*, 1930

interdependent. The Modern Merchandising Bureau was created, a company that acquired the rights to reproduce the scenic wardrobe used by movie stars, which were sold in a less expensive versions through Cinema Fashion, a chain also found in department stores. Meticulous Hollywood designers became consummate fashion pattern designers. Many even opened their own ateliers.

In 1930, the first attempts to create a national fashion took place in Italy. In Torino, the Ente Nazionalle della Moda (National Fashion Entity) was born. The political triumph of fascism led to an absolutist dictatorship, which favoured consuming only Italian products. The Mediterranean ideal of voluptuous, curvy beauty was preferred. The ideal physical type was the *Signorina grandi firme* (the Big Label Lady), an icon invented by Gino Boccasile for the cover of the magazine *Le grandi Firme*.

At the Lido, in Venice, chic ladies wore "day pajamas". The economic crisis influenced styles, with an unswerving return to austerity, and more fitted shapes were preferred. The breasts, waist and hips were again highlighted with more subtle and enveloping bias-cut clothes. These had to be put on over the head and offered a voluptuous image. Fabrics were subtle, light and fluid. Hems reached below the knee during the day and the ankle at night. For the morning, the complete three-piece suit was preferred: a skirt that opened with pleats or panels combined with a blouse and angora sweater and a three-quarter jacket. The waist returned with the use of belts with buckles, also worn with calf-length coats cut like a smoking jacket. Pleated inserts, tie collars or collars with kerchiefs, shawls and ribbons were common. The short bolero with shaped hems and embroidered embellishments returned. Women's

L. Venturi, Winter complete, Summer dress,
afternoon dress, 1939-1940

shoes were fastened with laces and a bow and had white inserts and punctured edges. In 1931, the Pants Brigade was born. This was an association founded to promote the now accepted comfortable trousers, which would evolve into a refined article with long legs, a high waist and pronounced pleats. The trouser suit was the garment of choice, with a jacket fitted at the waist and square shoulders. Marlene Dietrich, Carole Lombard and Katharine Hepburn wore this attire gracefully. Long and fitted evening gowns had a godet insert at the bottom and could include a small train. They were manufactured in cady, in dirty pastel hues or in ivory satin. Sliding over the silhouette, they contrasted with the naked skin revealed by the dramatic necklines on the back. Feminine seduction was entrusted to a mix of modesty and mystery, to which hats contributed, sometimes accessorized with veils. Headdresses were imaginative and increasingly smaller.

The shaped tailored line, a natural evolution of the straight coat, defined the front of the masculine silhouette. A grey flannel

Performers in the film *Stage Door*, 1937

THE HOLLYWOOD WARDROBE

Greta Garbo and Melvyn Douglas in *Ninotchka*, 1939

In the United States, the power of Hollywood grew. The colour of clothes assumed a symbolic value that communicated emotions. Designers played a fundamental role not only in the style of the divas on the set but in their private lives as well. Gilbert Adrian secured his place in the business by dressing Greta Garbo and Joan Crawford. Travis Banton took meticulous care of Marlene Dietriech's style: the white tuxedo, the rooster feathers' dress, the chiffon dress covered in gems. The magnetic look, the length of the hair (wavy and with barely defined curls that framed the face) as well as the use of a beret or turban transformed the celluloid heroine into a model for thousands of women. Other valued designers were Howard Freer, Edith Head and Orry Kelly, who was in charge of Bette Davis' image. Walter Plunkett created mostly period garments, designing the dresses of Scarlett O'Hara, portrayed by Vivien Leigh in Gone *With the Wind* (1939).

suit and vest was worn with a striped shirt of combed cotton and a whimsical silk necktie with a Windsor knot. The latest style was the V-shaped jacket, invented by Dutch tailor Frederic Scholte, which provided wider shoulders with respect to the rest of the body's structure and communicated a more physical type of elegance. The more modern wristwatch, initially used by pilots during the war, substituted the pocket watch. Their exquisite design made them one of the preferred new accessories, next to the silver cigarette case with engraved or enamelled initials and a pressure lock. The most common was a loose model with the right brim lifted, made of longhair felt and with a central crease. Two men admired for their impeccable elegance were the actor Clark Gable and the dancer Fred Astaire. In 1937, the first Rayban sunglasses with tinted lenses appeared.

The tennis polo shirt became an item. Created by tennis champion Renè Lacoste, it included a collar and was manufactured with a honeycomb piqué fabric. The textile sector underwent a true revolution. Unfaltering fabrics were used to produce intimate garments and bathing suits. The financial crisis forced everyone to economize and resort to artificial and synthetic fibres that did not require excessive maintenance. Important technological progress led to the large-scale use of new chemical dyes. Viscose (mixed with wool and cotton), acetate and Bemberg fabric (even and resistant and used for linings and nightgowns) began to be marketed. Aralac, a fibre extracted from the casein found in milk and similar to Merino wool, was an Italian autocratic specialty.

Albene, the first artificial opaque thread, was used in the manufacture of a soft, light satin called "peau d'ange" (angel's skin), suitable for the mermaid silhouette in dresses. While Madeleine Vionnet's bias cut "made history", nylon, synthesized from polymers and launched in 1938 by Dupont, was the true discovery of the period. Hard and elastic, crease-resistant and inexpensive, it

Fred Astaire and Ginger Rogers, 1930's

ACROSS THE SPORTS SCENE

ALIVE WITH COLOR AND CONVIVIALITY

The Ladies Home Journal, 1930

Chanel dress, 1938

Joan Crawford, *Sadie McKee*, 1934

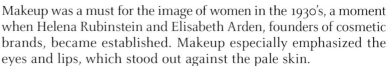

substituted silk and became the most used material for manufacturing transparent stockings that reached up to the mid thigh level and were fastened with garter belts. Surfaces were covered with regular shapes, symmetric or asymmetric, or were superimposed in vaguely cubist styles. Around the middle of the decade, floral motifs returned both for dresses and undergarments.

ICONS OF BEAUTY

Makeup was a must for the image of women in the 1930's, a moment when Helena Rubinstein and Elisabeth Arden, founders of cosmetic brands, became established. Makeup especially emphasized the eyes and lips, which stood out against the pale skin.

Max Factor, another giant in cosmetics, produced the pan-cake, a compact makeup base that concealed imperfections and was specifically created for actresses' faces. More and more, women resorted to jewellery cases for blusher, exhibiting them in public and flirting while powdering their noses. Lipstick was blood red; brows were waxed and reconfigured with a pencil into a subtle arched line, as in the case of platinum blonde Jean Harlow, who was catapulted to fame in Frank Capra's movie Platinum Blonde. Wide selections of dark shades were used on the eyelids while copious amounts of black mascara were used on long curved eyelashes (exaggerated false lashes). The hair had a sculpted cut, parted on the side, and large waves framed the face. Advances in chemistry allowed L'Oreal to offer various hair colours that were used by a multitude of women.

Illustration by Gino Boccasile, 1938-1939

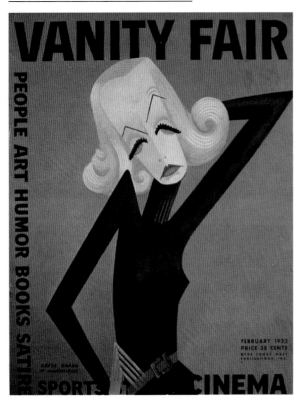

Miguel Covarrubias, cover of *Vanity Fair*, 1932

Salvatore Ferragamo, 1939

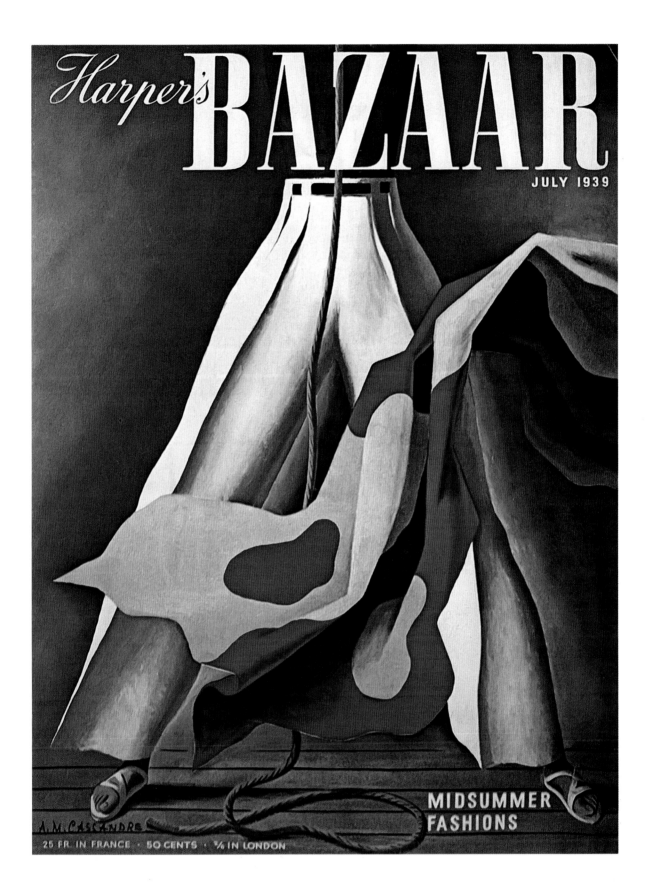

Illustration by Adolphe Mouron Cassandre,
1939

FASHION IN THE 1940s

THE WHITE TELEPHONE PERIOD

From 1939 to 1945 World War II, in which nations of all continents fought, threw the world into turmoil. The drama of the situation imposed great sacrifices in the face of all kinds of emergencies. Raw materials were in short supply because they were allocated for war purposes. Rationing included fabrics and garments as well, which shed any superfluous elements. In fashion, simplification prevailed, combined with tricks to hide daily difficulties. In the United States, magazines began a fight against waste and suggested that people "make do and mend", that is, readapt existing garments by adding modifications and giving them new life.

Curtains became wedding gowns; cut skirts became children's clothing, shawls and turbans; undergarments were made with linens. If a coat was worn out, it was turned inside out. The same held true with shirt collars and cuffs. Men's coats and suits were altered and used as women's tailored suits with square shoulders with shoulder pads in military style. Men's trousers became popular because they were practical. The wool from sweaters was recycled at home where leftover materials were used to make knitted clothes. Women used short cotton socks and orthopaedic

wedge shoes that left the big toe visible. Headscarves, hairnets and turbans reigned supreme, in part due to the shortage of electricity light that prevented the stylized hairdos that gave a woman's hair an impeccable appearance. Dressmaker Pauline Adam started the turban fashion, appropriating it from Simone de Beauvoir. There was no lack of ingenuity, however, when it came to dressing up. In the absence of stockings, legs were dyed with tea, chicory or walnut shells and the back seam was drawn with a pencil. Women's hats provided a creative release. Small, charming and imaginative, hats incorporated used scraps such as pieces of wood, paper and nets made of tulle.

In Paris, during the first yeas of the war, everything continued as before. Later, however, it was impossible to find luxury fabrics. Glass beads from Bohemia, for instance, could not be obtained because of the annexation of those territories by Germany. Many French ateliers closed while others moved abroad. With the German invasion in 1940, haute couture designs were devoted to the wives and lovers of Nazi officials, who led a privileged life thanks to their acquired power. German fashion for ordinary people suffered as a result of the sombre atmosphere that reigned in the country, one that imposed on women the image of the good mother devoted above all to patriotic fervour. The move to Berlin of the French fashion houses was avoided thanks to the patient diplomatic work of Lucien Lelong, the couturier who became president of the Chambre Syndicale de la Couture Parisienne (Paris' couture

One of the first post-war fashion shows in Milan, 1946

trade union). Talented designers such as Salvatore Ferragamo and embroiderer Lesage used inexpensive and alternative materials to create small works of art of rare genius. Twine, raffia, aluminium foil, newspaper, walnut shells and cork were some of the materials with which they sought to win the approval of their clientele and safeguard any semblance of newness and pizzazz in haute couture. In London, a designers' society was created in 1941, in which Norman Hartnell, Digby Morton, Victor Stiebel, Hardy Amies and Edward Molyneux participated, spearheading a national project for the basic definition of standardized cuts. These were utility garments: 32 models for serially produced functional garments. Many British factories adhered to the initiative and used the patterns, resulting in the democratization of shapes. Some of these factories were entrusted with designing women's British Army uniforms. Norman Hartnell created the uniforms for the Royal Air Force and the Red Cross. In Italy, fashion was defined by austerity and thrift, with a return to origins and a shift toward more traditional values. The fascist government not only prohibited imported

Scene from The Philadelphia Story, 1940

THE NEW LOOK
BY CHRISTIAN DIOR

In 1947, Christian Dior, then Lelong's collaborator, proposed, with the support of the French Syndicat de la Couture, a collection called "Corolle", which constituted an absolute novelty for the period and that would quickly be renamed the New Look. The style was directed toward the wealthy, stately and sophisticated woman. It extolled the female shape, with soft shoulders, emphasis on the bust, a subtle wasp's waist and a large skirt with fillings and godets that rounded the hips. The feminine and romantic look of Dior's creations was emphasized with details such as gloves, high heels, a purse and hat. For day dresses, the designer preferred simple lines that contrasted with

pronounced necklines, reserving the yards and yards of taffeta and tulle for evening gowns. He explored draping directly on the model. His favourite colours were white, black and pastels. The new length imposed by Dior was 25cm from the ground, resulting in the use of many yards of fine fabric ordered from silk factories in Lyon. The increase of textile production significantly helped re-launch the French fashion system and drew the attention of the international public to Paris.

Christian Dior, "Corolle" line, 1947

Popover dress, Claire McCardell, 1942

Left: Jacques Fath model of 1947,
Palais Galliera, Paris

items and imposed a rigorously autocratic form of consumption but also decided to eliminate all foreign terms in the vocabulary of fashion as well. Use of the *orbace*, a rustic, coarse wool fabric ideal for cold climates used as a blanket by shepherds in Sardinia, increased. Because of its consistency and impermeableness, this fabric was chosen for the winter uniforms of the Voluntary Militia for National Security, the famous "blackshirts" of the fascist leaders and some of the regime's youth organizations. Besides the use of artificial fibres, the production of broom, a native plant from which resistant but low-quality textile fibres could be extracted, was encouraged. In the United States, fashion suffered a setback during the war. The American War Production Board imposed a series of restrictions, though less severe than in Europe. Due to racial persecution, prominent Jewish families immigrated to the United States. British tailor Charles James moved his atelier to New York. Stylists such as Claire McCardell, Clare Potter, Jo Copeland and Muriel King, champions of American prêt-à-porter, proposed night dresses and knit bodysuits; comfortable suits and casual denim clothing with large pockets; shirt dresses, high-waist skirts and shorts made in cotton flannel. American women, endowed with a more practical mindset, particularly appreciated percale apron dresses. In California, fashion houses flourished, inspired by Hollywood designers and aspiring to highlight all the aspects of female charm. At the same time, in Paris, the Christian Dior's star burned brightly. The creator of the "new look" would imbue the fashion firmament and life with a new sense of excitement.

Bakelite purse

Jean Harlow

Rita Hayworth in *Gilda*, by Charles Vidor, 1946

Participants in the Miss Italy pageant, 1948

ICONS OF BEAUTY: RITA HAYWORTH

Rita Hayworth was the symbol of the decade. During World War II and the immediate post-war period, she embodied the quintessence of feminine beauty and was identified with erotic desire and the passion to live in spite of everything. Her natural Latin charm, highlighted by an impressive physique and a mane of thick wavy copper-coloured hair, was made use of in a series of successful films that transformed her into an authentic star. She played Gilda, a seductress with uncontrolled sensuality, in the eponymous film directed by Charles Vidor, which introduced the viewing public to famous musical numbers such as "Put the Blame on Mame" and Amado Mio. The striptease scene in which Hayworth, dressed in a bright black satin dress with a cut that revealed her exquisite legs, slowly and sensually delays the gesture of removing a sleeve retains mythical status to this day. In 1946, her picture was glued to the experimental atomic bomb launched on the Bikini Atoll, earning her the nickname "atomic".

FASHION IN THE 1950s

The 1950s were characterised by a strong sense of optimism for the future and the desire to leave behind the suffering and privations of the recently concluded war. Advertising became a successful strategy for the mass promotion of products launched onto the market. In opposition to traditional art, pop art firmly established itself with a series of artists that used consumer culture to introduce a popular form of art accessible to everyone. Utilitarian cars and vacations in fashionable places became widespread. New domestic appliances conceived to lighten the household tasks of women, who longed without exception to embody the "ideal woman", a sophisticated, perfumed and impeccable housewife managing a sweet refuge for her "warrior", were acquired with certain euphoria. For important

Left: Gattinoni, 1952, in the Colloseum, Rome
Below: Irene Galitzine, 1954, bridal collection

occasions almost all women wanted to wear a mink coat and have their nails and lips painted red, as the privileges of the rich now seemed more accessible. It is said that Elizabeth Taylor, aware of the media power of colours, secured for herself the exclusive use of red lipstick on the set, prohibiting its use by other actresses. Investments in movies and Hollywood productions began to be made again. Through diving and sports, models of behaviour inspired by the American dream returned, for everything that came from across the ocean was embraced with enthusiasm. The Actors' Studio was formed in New York, with a generation of new actors. In 1954, Marilyn Monroe appeared in *How To Marry a Millionaire*, bringing to the screen a candid sensuality wrapped in a dress that accentuated her perfect curves. In the movie *The Seven Year Itch* (1955), designer William Travilla dressed her in a pleated white dress with a wide sash at the waist and a halter neck. In one scene, an air current from the subway lifts her skirt, revealing Marilyn's lovely legs in a pair of stiletto heels. The American style of dress became more functional. The general use of comfortable and easy-to-wear cotton fibres and knit garments grew, while the use of synthetic fibres that dried quickly and did not require too much care became widespread.

Advertisement for linen

Left: Coco Chanel, tailored suit, 1954

Yves Saint Laurent for Christian Dior, trapeze dress, 1958

Emilio Schuberth, 1950

VOGUE

SEPTEMBER 15.

The New Way:
to be in fashion
and stay
an individual

Vogue, 1955, cover by John Rawlings

Left: Christian Dior, *new look*, 1956

Emilio Schubert, 1953

Sorelle Fontana, 1952

Fashion took inspiration from the world of youth culture, and garments designed for young people represented a flourishing market in expansion. Blue jeans, closefitting pants made of blue denim fabric, appeared. They would become one of the most important fashion phenomena of the 20th century. Used until the middle of the 20th century as work clothes on account of their durability, they were worn by miners and labourers, had wide pockets for holding tools and were reinforced with a double seam and metal rivets. After the success of films such as *The Wild One* (1953), starring Marlon Brando, and *Rebel Without A Cause* (1955), starring James Dean, blue jeans, combined with a t-shirt and leather jacket, were embraced by American university students as an emblem of a new rebellious and restless generation. Men and young people replaced ankle boots with leather moccasins (inspired by native American footwear) with a band, high tongue and leather heel, which became the preferred footwear of Ivy League students.

In France, the ideas of the philosopher Jean-Paul Sartre inspired the movement of the young existentialists, who wore tight black sweaters and pants, listened to songs by Juliette Greco and cultivated an air of radical and chic intellectuals. In England, small groups of "teddy boys" formed. A working class youth subculture, the "teddy boys" were intent on imitating the style that was in vogue during the Edwardian period, recreated by Saville Row tailors after

Brunetta, Jole Veneziani, 1951

Left: Roberto Capucci, 1953

THE BIRTH OF ITALIAN FASHION

Carosa, 1950

With the help of the most accredited American buyers, Gian Battista Giorgini organized a fashion show featuring 170 day, afternoon, cocktail and evening dresses, created by Simonetta, Fabiani, Sorelle Fontana, Emilio Schubert, Carosa (Princess Giovanna Caracciolo) of Rome; Germana Maruccelli, Iole Veneziani, Noberasco and Vanna di Milano, designers who had consolidated their own style instead of copying French models. Emilio Pucci, Avolio, Bertoli and Tessitrice dell'Isola participated in boutique fashion with sports lines accessories. The show was a huge success and brought attention to "Made in Italy" designs, the freshness of which won the favour of the public. The famous American daily WWD (Women's Wear Daily) covered the event enthusiastically. From that moment on, Italian fashion was introduced in a series of organized events, first in the Grand Hotel and later in the Sala Bianca in Palazzo Pitti, in Florence (1952). It unleashed the high quality of elegant fibres, fabrics and handmade applications of coral, mother-of-pearl and cabochon. Italian dresses venerated aesthetic models that respected the natural proportions of the figure and were adapted elegantly and harmoniously to the customization of feminine tastes.

Previous page: Sorelle Fontana, 1952

Below: Poster for Sorelle Fontana, 1956

World War II. They wore long corduroy jackets with shoulder pads, drainpipe trousers, pointy-toed shoes and colourful socks. Shirts were worn with the collar up to reveal a striped Slim Jim tie. The "teddy boy" hairstyle consisted of a duck's tail in the back and a heavily pomaded quiff that fell over the forehead.

Around the middle of the decade, the couture house Brioni, founded in Florence in 1952, introduced men's continental-style clothing adapted to a cosmopolitan and international clientele. These garments included short, straight, slightly closefitting jackets with simple buttons that followed the natural lines of the body with vaguely defined shoulders and pants without cuffs. Often they were combined with vests of the same material with pockets and a half belt in the back, an essential garment, particularly in winter. The Brioni shirt was impeccable, featuring a classic cut. As accessories, men wore a large white neckerchief with stripes on the edges and a fanciful silk tie.

Paris haute couture, an expression of the most opulent luxury fabrics, accessories and perfumes, experienced a resurgence thanks to the creative genius of Christian Dior, who emphasised femininity to the maximum and launched two collections a year in a such way that the preceding ones became immediately obsolete. Due to his international success, Dior was invited to the United States to promote the serial production of his creations. Meanwhile, Paris continued dictating standards. Ateliers, dressmakers' shops and editorial desks were concentrated on Avenue Matignon. Chanel, Jean Lanvin, Cristobal Balenciaga, Pierre Balmain, Nina Ricci, Jacques Fath, Elsa Schiaparelli and Madame Paquin dressed the most elegant and richest women in the world in custom-made garments exquisitely cut in precious and exclusive materials. Tasteful finishes, silk lining and meticulously executed details contributed to the survival of the myth of Paris chic. Some of the most important collections created by Christian Dior, who had been working since 1957, found inspiration in the shape of corollas, tulips and letters

Left: Dresses by Jean Dessès, 1955 and
Cristóbal Balenciaga, 1958, Galliera Museum,
Paris

Above: Mme. Grés, 1956-57, Galliera Museum,
Paris

of the alphabet: his I-, H-, A- and Y-lines. Evening gowns reached the feet and were complemented with boleros or fur stoles and long tight-fitting gloves. Shoes had pointy toes, buckles made of precious stones and a high heel. Stockings were transparent and of flesh-coloured nylon. Roger Vivier was Dior's preferred supplier of sandals and evening footwear. The Dior handbag was satin, in contrast to the clothes and shoes. The accessories worn by society women, as dictated by convention, were always coordinated and tonally complementary with their makeup. At that time, René Gruau was one of the best fashion illustrators. The period saw the return of the integrated corset, which narrowed the waist and highlighted the hips, and the *guepière*, a kind of bustier invented by Marcel Rochas, was used. Bras had reinforced cups with filling to give the impression of ample cleavage. Coco Chanel, a woman with a strong personality, remained faithful to her own ideas and detested Dior's dresses, which she dismissed as stiff and uncomfortable. She reopened her atelier and introduced a tailored suit in extravagant boucle fabric, of pastel tones, with a straight or slightly evase skirt, collarless jacket, pockets, edged borders with passementerie and jewel buttons. In 1957, Dior surprised everyone again with the launch of his line of *sack* dresses, causing quite a stir due to the fact that they totally concealed the waist, subverting the rules in force at the time. When Coco Chanel died, Yves Saint Laurent replaced her as the director of the Chanel fashion house. At his debut, in continuity with the sack dresses, he launched his trapeze dress, a fresh and youthful collection that met with overwhelming success. The most famous fashion photographers of the period were Irving Penn, John French and Richard Avedon. Women's magazines multiplied, offering all sorts of advice to anyone interested in enhancing their style. Ordinary women, who did not have the means to obtain such costly designs, were forced to copy the proposals seen in the photographs of fashion magazines with help of mannequins or they sought the services of a dressmaker to the fashion the garments. The weddings of kings and queens, magnified by the media, contributed

Valentino, 1958

Right: Model with dress by Federico Forquet
on the streets of Rome, 1959

to creating the myth of the fairy tale couple: Queen Elizabeth and the Prince of Edinburgh; Grace Kelly and Prince Ranier; Soraya and the Shah of Iran; Rita Hayworth and Aga Khan; Fabiola and Balduin of Belgium; and, finally, Jacqueline Bouvier and John F. Kennedy. Italian designers still looked to French couture for inspiration, importing creations from the Parisian runways and adding nods and winks to the Renaissance and the 19th century. The unquestionable dominance of French fashion began to be challenged on 12 February 1951, when the Marquis Gian Battista Giorgini organised the first official presentation of Italian models at his Florentine villa. The dresses featured a subtle waist and a wide, long skirt that highlighted the breasts, underscored by elements embroidered with curled gold or silver thread, beads and sequins that repeated at the bottom of the diaphanous skirt. Eveningwear generously revealed the shoulders with plunging necklines in the open back and front. The use of organdie, moaré, silk faille, satin, damask, taffeta, velvet, tulle and lace, along with new rayon fabrics and short printed viscose fibres, highly appreciated in foreign markets, was common. Each material was carefully selected depending on the day and the occasion. Textile manufacturers experimented with new fibres such as lilion, orlon and acetate, which would evolve in the 1960s. The relationship between fashion and film grew increasingly close.

Models posing in Campidoglio fashion spread in *European magazine*, Rome, 1955

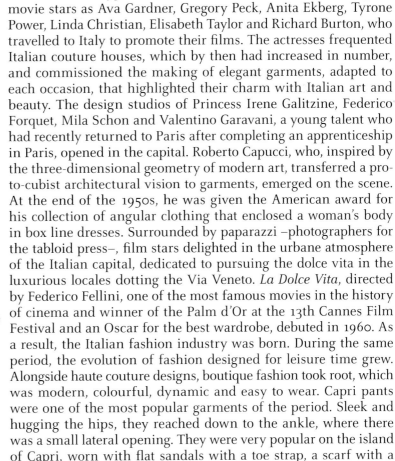

In the mid-1950s, Rome welcomed such celebrated American movie stars as Ava Gardner, Gregory Peck, Anita Ekberg, Tyrone Power, Linda Christian, Elisabeth Taylor and Richard Burton, who travelled to Italy to promote their films. The actresses frequented Italian couture houses, which by then had increased in number, and commissioned the making of elegant garments, adapted to each occasion, that highlighted their charm with Italian art and beauty. The design studios of Princess Irene Galitzine, Federico Forquet, Mila Schon and Valentino Garavani, a young talent who had recently returned to Paris after completing an apprenticeship in Paris, opened in the capital. Roberto Capucci, who, inspired by the three-dimensional geometry of modern art, transferred a proto-cubist architectural vision to garments, emerged on the scene. At the end of the 1950s, he was given the American award for his collection of angular clothing that enclosed a woman's body in box line dresses. Surrounded by paparazzi –photographers for the tabloid press–, film stars delighted in the urbane atmosphere of the Italian capital, dedicated to pursuing the dolce vita in the luxurious locales dotting the Via Veneto. *La Dolce Vita*, directed by Federico Fellini, one of the most famous movies in the history of cinema and winner of the Palm d'Or at the 13th Cannes Film Festival and an Oscar for the best wardrobe, debuted in 1960. As a result, the Italian fashion industry was born. During the same period, the evolution of fashion designed for leisure time grew. Alongside haute couture designs, boutique fashion took root, which was modern, colourful, dynamic and easy to wear. Capri pants were one of the most popular garments of the period. Sleek and hugging the hips, they reached down to the ankle, where there was a small lateral opening. They were very popular on the island of Capri, worn with flat sandals with a toe strap, a scarf with a

triangular knot and a straw handbag. The version that reached the middle of the calf, called clam-diggers or pirate pants, were perfectly suited for dancing to rock and roll, an attractive alternative to the wide, circular, knee-length skirt that made pirouettes. The bikini, a two-piece bathing suit that leaves the bellybutton visible and owes it name to the nuclear tests on the Bikini Atoll, appeared on fashionable beaches. One of the first to wear one was a stunning and very young Bridgette Bardot on the sunny shores of Saint Tropez, the launching place of the latest trends. Pants were not worn in summer only but for sports and skiing as well, in versions with a band below the heel and tight trouser legs. Emilio Pucci, a Florentine noble who was passionate about sports, began his career in the world of fashion after *Harper's Bazaar* photographer Toni Frissel discovered one of his ski outfits on the slopes of Saint Moritz. The Pucci style, straight silk shirts printed in bright colours based on the idea of the scarf with hem, became synonymous with the refined elegance of "Made in Italy". Knit, considered a material of little value, also assumed a place in fashion collections as an elegant proposal for daily life. Emilio Pucci, whose nickname was the "restless Marquis", experimented with sweaters made of polyester and silk organdie.

ICONS OF BEAUTY AND ELEGANCE

While beauty contests to elect the various Misses multiplied, the prototype of the pin-up, the ideal woman that emerged in 1943 with Jane Russell, wearing a bullet bra designed by Howard Hughes, became popular. The sumptuous woman with a wasp waist and

FILMS

The Girls of the Spanish Steps (1953), Luciano Emmer

How To Marry A Millionaire (1954), Jean Negulesco

The Seven Year Itch (1955), Billy Wilder

Roman Holiday (1953), William Wyler

Quadrophenia (1979), Franc Roddam

Rebel Without A Cause (1955), Nicholas Ray

The Wild One (1953), László Benedek

La Dolce Vita (1960), Federico Fellini

Blue Hawaii (1961), Norman Taurog

ample hips and breasts had perfect measurements: 90, 60, 90, like those of Silvana Mangano in the movie *Mambo*. Lucia Bosé, Gina Lollobrigida and Sofia Loren embodied the seductive model of Mediterranean beauty: healthy and carnal, spontaneous, typical of post-war Italy. The breasts were the focal point that caught the eye. In parallel, a new image of female beauty, fresher and more natural, that used pastel colours and more discreet tones, emerged. Blonde Grace Kelley, an actress of aristocratic demeanour and a favourite of Alfred Hitchcock, was the manifestation of impeccable, poised and sober elegance. For her, Hermès would create the Kelly-bag, a small leather purse that closed with a combination lock. In stark contrast to this was Brigitte Bardot, a French fashion model with a childish expression who combined naiveté and sensuality, expressing an unprecedented type of eroticism: the "girl-child". Often with uncombed hair or her hair worn in a dishevelled up style, she appeared in jumpsuits with a balcony neckline made of Vichy cotton flannel or Sangallo cloth, awakening the disapproval of moralists for her non-conformist behaviour.

The ideal synthesis of the imposing woman with a touch of naiveté was Marilyn Monroe, one of the public's favourite stars, who at night would wear only five drops of Chanel no. 5. A sex symbol imitated by countless women, who, like her, dyed their hair platinum blond and fashioned their eyebrow arch to look like a

Brigitte Bardot, 1950

Actress Sylvia Koscina with Capucci, 1958

Grace Kelly, 1954

"seagull's wing", the diva's perfectly applied makeup was the result of careful study, obtained in a daily three-hour session. While in private life Marilyn might have preferred jeans, in the movies she appeared sheathed in dresses that accentuated her curves and wore mesh stockings and tight sweaters that called attention to her breasts, a garment that Lana Turner, nicknamed "the Sweater Girl", would also adopt. Meanwhile, Audrey Hepburn had doe eyes, thick brows and the innocent and fresh air of a well-mannered girl. Her favourite designer, both on the screen and in private life, was Hubert de Givenchy.

FASHION IN THE 1960s

In the 1960s, the silhouette became more subtle and elongated. A certain geometry of forms prevailed. Simplicity of line was sought following modern tastes but without sacrificing the refinement of traditional style. The artisanal production of garments, with tests, was reserved for haute couture, which produced unique pieces designed with the customer's body in mind. Thanks to the company Snia Viscosa, the production of artificial and synthetic fibres abounded (obtained through extrusion, they were the result of chemical and technological research and were highly regarded by Italian haute couture during its international rise). Delphion, lilion, Trevira, silene, dialen, Bemberg, perlon, Tricel, dorian and ortalion are some of the materials that were used to make lace, brocades, laminates, organdie, taffeta, chiffon and padding, while embroidery on garments tended to disappear. Italian style made a qualitative jump. In 1961, Pino Lancetti inaugurated his design shop with a haute couture collection that combined prêt-à-porter lines, leatherworking and accessories. In 1963, he launched his "military line". Inspired by contemporary art, Lancetti designed opulent prints in surprising shades of colour, and for this reason was called a "tailor painter". Straight-lined evening gowns with a halter neck, often adorned with sensational inlays and embroidery

Norman Norell, 1965

Roberta di Camerino, 1965

Irene Galitzine, photograph of Johnny Moncada, *Italian Line*, s/s 1967,
© Johny Moncada Archive

THE MINISKIRT

The miniskirt represented a genuine fashion revolution and is considered a symbol of feminine liberation. Leaving the legs bare, an essential element in female seduction, it suggested sexual freedom and uninhibited behaviour that challenged the social system. *The Sunday Times* defined 1963 as the "year of legs". Inspired by the skirts of English school uniforms, the miniskirt spread rapidly and became the mainstay of a new generation, arousing the indignation of the defenders of public morality. The measurements of the miniskirt varied: from 15 cm above the knew with a cuff at the middle of the thigh, a length tolerated even in the most aristocratic environments such as the English court, to a minimum length that barely covered the buttocks, considered by many to be an affront to modesty. The miniskirt owes its good fortune, above all, to the high level of acceptance among men, but also to the enthusiasm with which designers embraced a novelty that required fewer centimetres of cloth than the traditional skirt and allowed for good profit margins. Mary Quant is considered the inventor of the miniskirt, which she combined with the "skinny rib", a sweater that stuck to the ribs and squashed together the breasts. However, its parentage is also attributed to Andrè Courréges and John Bates, who introduced among their designs garments unmistakably "mini" in the same year.

Brigitte Bardot in a miniskirt, 1960s

with bead necklaces, jais, little tubes and beading, were painstaking and skilful works of art.

Among the most highly regarded creators of Italian haute couture were Iole Veneziani, Biki, o Galitzine, Gattinoni, Mila Schon, Raffaella Curiel, Fausto Sarli, Renato Balestra and Rocco Barocco. Especially noteworthy is Valentino, who, in 1967, launched his "V" logo as a decorative motif for a tin buckle, repeating this element on the pockets of a white wool coat. In 1968 he dedicated a series of garments from his "white collection" to Jacqueline Kennedy, from among which she chose the design for her wedding with Aristotle Onassis. In March of the same year, Valentino opened his first boutique in Paris; in 1967, the crucial role of the city of art, where promotional events were concentrated and organized, was established. Rome would become the headquarters of haute couture fashion shows, while Florence was reserved for the boutique and luxury prêt-à-porter fashion market, always in higher demand. Among the middle class, the use of "good" tailored suit, durable and used only on special occasions, spread. Always in Italy, the presence of Roberta di Camerino, who created beautiful three-dimensional prints for the shirtdresses of elegant women, was felt. The designer transferred the *trompe-l'oeil* technique to fashion, inserting false collars and cuffs in sweaters or pockets and belts of contrasting colours in long printed polyester dresses. American designer Ken Schott, the "gardener of fashion", opened a boutique in Milan. His style is a whirlwind of peonies, roses, poppies, sunflowers, petunias and stars. Enamoured with nature and colours, he disseminated *imprimè* made in the print shops of Como on shirtdresses, shirts, beach outfits, bikinis, stockings and scarves. The whimsical nature of the silk organdie garments by Emilio Pucci became increasingly more stylised, and his production

Page from *Vanity Fair*, 1960

licenses included belts, suitcases, glasses and perfumes. Pucci made fashionable the coordinated bag and scarf and the Bermunda pants and blouse combination that famous women such as Jacqueline Onassis embraced. The overarching patterns of the prints – apart from plant and geometric motifs such as strips, squares and chevrons – were diffuse fantasies such as marblized or mottled surfaces. In 1966, the Flora design, dedicated to Grace of Monaco and applied to the famous Gucci silk scarves, appeared. Vittorio Accornero was responsible for their execution, with nine flower bouquets from all the seasons, wild berries, butterflies, dragonflies and insects painted with enchanting mystery. The emerging creative model was inspired by the myth of youth: instead of following in the footsteps of their parents, young people experienced a generational conflict and searched for new attitudes in opposition to the demands of the middle class family and took advantage of consumer society, as Andy Warhol did in the arts. They also imposed their tastes in dress styles through provocative garments. Fashion arose from the innovative agitation of the street, from King's Road and Carnaby Street, famous London meeting places. Countercultural expressions or youth movements such as mods and rockers emerged from pubs and taverns where the first rock and roll groups began to play. In the shop windows of Bazar (Mary Quant boutique that opened in 1955) and Biba (opened in 1964), garments paid no attention to the prejudices inherent in sex, age and social conditions, while millions of young people began to imitate the images and attitudes of their idols. For the first time in a long time, young men let their hair and beards grow long. They wore shirts and ties with flowers on them and Nehru jackets, inspired by the Liverpool four, the mythical Beatles, who had bowl-cropped hair with bangs. In 1965 Elizabeth II of England honoured them with the title of members of the British Royal Order. The Beatles had their photographs taken

Hiroko Matsumoto for Pierre Cardin, 1966

Emilio Pucci, 1966

BARBIE, "THE MODERN DOLL"

In 1959, the first Barbie, "the modern doll" with an adult appearance, appeared in the United States. Barbie had a long, linear figure, long legs, narrow waist, large breasts and detailed facial features. Made of vinyl, it was manufactured by Mattel. Barbie represented an unprecedented sales phenomenon: in 1959, 350 million units were sold at three dollars a piece. The wild success was due in large part to the brilliant intuition to market a doll with garments and accessories that were sold separately. In 1961 Ken, Barbie's boyfriend, appeared, with relatives and friends being added over time.

Through Barbie, girls were introduced to the worship/game of fashion from a young age and learned to care for their appearance using a series of accessories included with the doll.

THE BEATLES

in narrow, closefitting coats, tight, short pants and black leather ankle boots. Later, they flew to India in search of inspiration and adopted a more extravagant style, including garments inspired by the military uniforms of the period (they expressed their disagreement with the Vietnam War, which had begun in 1964), oriental kaftans, velvet scarves, frilly shirts, hook vests, necklaces and rings. While the countercultural generation mounted protests on the campus of Berkeley University, in California, which were as contagious as the obstinate rhythms of the Rolling Stones, London, New York and San Francisco became the capitals of fashion for teenagers (ages 13 to 19). The Stones had a more rebellious style than the Beatles and an angry expression emphasized by their dishevelled hair. Strident colours, bright fabrics, velvet pants and satin shirts, leather jackets with hippy-style fringes, once forbidden for the "stronger" sex for so long now widely replaced the grey uniform of the good boy from a middle class home, opening the door to unisex garments. Teenage girls aspired to an unconventional identity, used contraceptives and embraced the image of the Chelsea girl, adopting the rebellious miniskirt with their uncovered legs sheathed in opaque in the first elastic pantyhose. Alongside

a fashion style bursting with colours, the creation of one's own personal style was completed with facial makeup that centred on the eyes, remarkable through the use of eyeliner pencil and black mascara and accentuated with fake eyelashes, used in several layers or in strips to create a "doll" effect. Faded blue or green shadows in the arch of the brow added brightness to the gaze. Lipstick colours recalled children's lips: pastel pink, coral or lavender. Young women's hairstyles were short and asymmetrical like the Vidal Sassoon shape or bowl cuts with bangs. Carded hair was still worn, gathered with a band or in a ponytail. More free time and money transformed the new generation into consumers that were highly valued by the production system. Young women wore the tube dress, which merged with the figure, or dresses with trapezoidal lines, or sack dresses, such as the one that Cristobal Balenciaga and Hubert de Givenchy, astute observers of social phenomena, rushed to present on French fashion runways. The tube dress caresses the body. Made of jersey fabric or stiff synthetic or acrylic material, it had a tailored fit with double stitching, inserts and contrasting borders. Some of the most noteworthy materials were Lurex and hides and skins, which were treated to give them a bright and scintillating effect. Bright, shrill colours and graphic elements on flat surfaces were predominant. Coats and outer garments became more playful: trapezoid-shaped, narrow at the top and bell-shaped below and knee length. The wearer's age was not important. Yves Saint Laurent was among the first to incorporate into official fashion the non-conformist aspirations of society, which also exerted a strong influence on fashion runways. After his 1960 collection "Beat Look", with black leather jackets and turtleneck sweaters, and the debut of his first independent collec-

tion, in 1961, inspired by the Existentialists, in 1965 he created the modernist-style white-knit tube dresses such as the "Mondrian dress" and vinyl raincoats that took everyone by surprise. 1966 was the year of the pantsuit and woman's tuxedo. In 1968 unisex garments appeared, including the famous safari-style Saharan garment and transparent, short and long "nude look" garments. Among his most elegant and wearable designs were the shirtdress, preferred by more traditional women, with canesú in back and a masculine collar, buttoned cuffs and double pockets and lapels – an updated version of the silk shirtdress – which reached to the knee and was adorned with a belt and jewel buttons. Pierre Cardin was readmitted into the Chambre Syndicale de la Haute Couture, from which he had been expelled in 1959 after launching in Paris a collection for the large Printemps department stores. Soon he, too, was presenting innovative designs for men: pants and a collar-less slim corduroy jacket; jackets with a belt, high Korean-style collar and hidden buttons; tight suits like the jumpsuits worn by astronauts, with a zipper (in the absence of traditional pockets and buttons) combined with a knit polo shirt with a high collar that replaced the dress shirt. Girls preferred the low-waist pichi, a sleeveless garment designed for wearing on top of a blouse or closefitting canalé sweater, which was tightened with a belt at the hip. Due to their resemblance to a work apron, some variants of this model were also worn in the home. Lengths rose vertiginously above the knee, and the collections of Dorothée Bis and Sonia Rykie consisted of fast fashion, carefree mini-garments that lent adolescent charm.

Designers found new sources of inspiration in pop art and optical art. André Courrèges, who in 1964 launched the spatial line with Audrey Hepburn and Twiggy and who reasserted the invention of the miniskirt, proposed optical fashion, inspired by the English artist Bridget Riley, an important figure in the movement. Like

Twiggy, cover of *Vogue*, July 1967

THE NUDE LOOK

While the protests placed emphasis on an increased awareness of one's own self, already in 1964, on the beaches of Saint Tropez, naked breast fashion, which preceded the appearance of the one-piece swimsuit in place of the bikini, was common. This new custom celebrated the freedom of the body that transparent materials called attention to. In the late 1960s, Courrèges presented organdie dresses with floral or geometric applications that covered the intimate areas. *The Times* reported on the scandal caused by the designer Federico Forquet, who dressed one of his models in red crepé skirt and plastic-ring and coral necklaces with her chest bare. To make the "see-not-see" designs more wearable, a series of semi-transparent muslin shirts adorned with flounces and pleats that fell over the breasts and enhanced the sleeves were launched. Different versions that won the favour of many women appeared on the market. In the winter of 1968, Yves Saint Laurent, considered the genius of the period, presented a long black completely transparent muslin dress with ostrich feather applications on the thighs and hips. A gold belt in the shape of a snake completed this tremendously sensual outfit.

Yves Saint Laurent, 1968

Paco Rabanne, 1960

Courrèges, Ossie Clark in London and Yves Saint Laurent in Paris created models characterised by optical effects in black and white with repeated geometric patterns to create three-dimensional effects. The optical images, which the created the illusion of movement, became the most widespread trend along with the use of boots. Spaniard Paco Rabanne, nicknamed the "metallurgist of fashion", invented a garment made of metal plates – inspired by the armour of warriors – joined with rings and worn against the bare skin. The clothing of the film *Barbarella*, based on the comic book by Jean-Claude Forest and starring an audacious Jane Fonda, are his. Toward the end of the 1960s, the discussion concerning the length of the skirt became even more polemical. In 1967, following the success of the film Doctor Zhivago, the military-style maxi coat with a large fur hat became fashionable, and suits where mini and maxis coexisted in the same outfit appeared on magazine covers. A middle ground was sought with the invention of the midi, which fell to the middle of the calf, though it was not particularly flattering.

PHOTOGRAPHERS AND MODELS

While Andy Warhol painted the most representative beauties of his time, fixing them forever in the collective memory, the new female stereotypes to imitate were the models that appeared in the magazines of the star system. They were flat-chested, with very long legs and silky voluminous hair. Twiggy, who had an ephebic and juvenile look, and was practically anorexic, was the first to attain such unimaginable fame. She became famous because of her rebellious boy hairstyle, her extremely large made-up eyes and a space between her front teeth that transformed her into the "new face" of "swinging London". The nickname "Twiggy" is an explicit reference to her adolescent thinness. Mary Quant decided to use her to launch the miniskirt. She appeared as an actress and singer in the movie *The Boy Friend* (1971), directed by Ken Russell; on the cover of the album *Pin Ups* (1973) by David Bowie; and in the film *The Blues Brothers* (1980). Diane Arbus photographed Penelope Tree, great-granddaughter of Marshall Field, founder of the department stores Marshall Field and Company of Chicago, when she was 13. She appeared in public in the "dance in black and white" organized by Truman Capote, wearing a long black dress with a low-cut "V" neckline that made her a pop icon. A regular on the London hippy scene, she began to work with photographers Cecil Beaton, Richard Avedon and David Bailey. Jean Shrimpton, called "The Shrimp", had a fragile and elegant air to her and appeared on the covers of *Vogue*, *Harper's Bazaar* and *Vanity Fair* at the age of 18. In 1965, in a short dress, designed by Colin Rolfe , which The Shrimp wore during the Victoria Derby, she attracted the attention of the media. In 1967 she was chosen to act in the film *Privilege* by Peter Watkins, alongside Paul Jones. The extremely tall Veruschka, launched by Johnny Moncada, became one of the most important supermodels of the period. She appeared as herself in the film *Blow-Up* by Michelangelo Antonioni (1966), set in swinging London. Along with her work in fashion, she offered her body to experimental body paint procedures. The movie *Who Are You, Polly Maggoo?* by William Klein raises the question of personal identity with respect to the sweetened image provided by fashion magazines. It is the story of a famous top model persecuted by her admirers, who reproach her for being, in their view, unreal, and by a television crew intent on dissecting every moment of her life.

Emilio Schuberth; model Birgitta af Klercker; photo, Johnny Moncada © Johnny Moncada Archive

Antonelli; model, Veruscka; *Harper's Bazaar
UK*, September 1963

The photographs on these 2 pages are by
Johnny Moncada © Johnny Moncada Archive

Irene Galitzine; model, Veruscka; *Harper's
Bazaar* (United Kingdom), September 1963

Garnett; model, Birgitta af Klercker;
Italian line, 1967-68

Irene Galitzine; model Veruscka; *Harper's Bazaar* (United Kingdom), September 1963

Lancetti; model, Veruscka; *Harper's Bazaar* (United Kingdom), September 1964

Pierre Cardin; model, Hiroto; *The Tatler*, February 1963

ICONS OF ELEGANCE

Audrey Hepburn and Catherine Deneuve embodied the Parisian style, and Deneuve remained loyal to the fashion creations of Yves Saint Laurent. Both marked a decisive shift in feminine elegance, with the affirmation of a svelte figure and a calm and modern classicism. Meanwhile, the enchanting sophistication of Jacqueline Kennedy – who on official occasions wore tailored suits and pillbox hats with matching coats made especially for her by the American designer Oleg Cassini – tended toward a new, more democratic and casual notion of femininity: large black sunglasses, scarves knotted beneath the chin, linear pants of sober, subdued colours, and Chanel-style striped t-shirts.

FASHION IN THE 1970s

The 1970s began in an atmosphere of new values that a society in transformation had expressed in the wake of 1968's cultural revolution. In this tense climate, the Vietnam War broke out, and in reaction to it, the "flower power" pacifist movement in the United States, founded by the "flower children", young hippies that professed an alternative culture and lived in communes, emerged. The movement, linked to the slogan "Make love, not war", deplored private property and proposed a complete subversion of the social order, often resorting to the use of psychedelic drugs in order to open doors of consciousness and perception of new horizons and sensations. "Peace & Love" was the universally known logo printed on t-shirts and emblems, on metal to be transformed into necklaces, on medallions or on belt buckles. The most representative cult movies of the period were *Easy Rider* (1969), directed by and starring Dennis Hopper and Peter Fonda and Jack Nicholson, and Zabriskie Point (1970) by Michelangelo Antonioni. Young people were passionate about contact with nature and a macrobiotic diet. They went on adventures, taking off with their backpacks to discover ethnic groups and places that were uncontaminated by progress; they appreciated folklore products and local crafts. Many sexual barriers fell; taboos that had limited the fluidity of relations between the sexes vanished. Fashion became infected with this demand for novelty, emerging as the privileged vehicle, next to music, for the definitive consolidation of radical and sudden social changes. Hippies adopted wild shocks of hair, psychedelic makeup, flashy colours, giant fantastical flowers, long kaftans and ethnic necklaces and trinkets. They freely mixed mini-skirts, transpar-

Poster of the film Easy Rider

Musical *Hair*

214

ent Indian tunics, military garments, frayed bellbottoms, velvet coats, Moroccan slippers and ethnic handbags with little mirrors, striped vests, leather boots, exotic hats, beaded belts, patchwork shirts, shapeless handmade sweaters, Franciscan sandals, Afghan leather jackets with Mongolian embroideries and silk scarves with batik prints. From the point of view of consumption, the contrast between generations became more acute. The feminist movement of that time as well, because of its rejection of the objectification of women, identified with long cotton flannel skirts with frills, grandmother's lingerie with lace trimmings, wide crochet shawls and heavy Dutch clogs. The result was a multifarious and eccentric ensemble, a sort of anti-fashion statement with a gypsy and dishevelled air that almost always resorted to second hand clothes. On the British scene, singer David Bowie appeared, the embodiment

Jane Fonda, *Klute*, 1971

At Stintino beach, Sardinia, August 1974

of glam rock (or glitter rock), a musical genre whose name derives from the use of a glamorous attire of great theatrical effect, extroverted, irreverent and ostentatious. Also in London, the loudspeaker of youth's cultural interests, punk was born, in 1976, becoming a fashion phenomenon thanks to Vivienne Westwood. The old rules of good manners and etiquette gave way to casual behaviour. Also among adults, a reaction against the uniformity of tastes imposed by the standardization of the production of clothes took place. Men and women used the same fitted shapes, long bell-shaped jackets with large lapels, low-rise bellbottom trousers and Borsalino hats. Pants suit of velvet, tweed or silk crepe (for the afternoon) with a silk shirt and bow collar became a symbol of the entrepreneurial and always elegant woman. The most significant designer of the period was Yves Saint Laurent, a cultivated and passionate collector who, in 1966, had opened Rive Gauche, a chain of fast and inexpensive fashion stores. A profound innovator of women's clothing, he adapted traditionally masculine garments such as the tuxedo, raincoat, baggy trousers, safari jacket and pants suit for women. Men's attire began to embrace colours and fanciful fabrics with small motifs for jackets and pastel hues for shirts, while the size of neckties grew, becoming wide and colourful like the kipper, designed by Michael Fish in his Picadilly shop. Lauren launched a new line of clothes. Casual but aristocratic, they took their inspiration from English countryside. Along with Calvin Klein, he explored an easy elegance, both feminine and masculine, that ultimately led to the notion of "casual

luxury". For both sexes, the wool coordinated set, available in a wide range of variations, was presented as garments that could be combined and that came in different colours and fabrics.

The "do it yourself" trend allowed for a more subjective vision that freed itself from the old dictates imposed from above. Women wore layer after layer of knitwear: skirts, t-shirts with cuffs, polo shirts, turtlenecks, pullovers, cardigans, long vests, capes and ponchos with hoods. The protagonists of this trend were Mariuccia Mandelli, known as Krizia, and Missoni, true prêt-à-porter pioneers. Their simple and casual designs were preferred because they were comfortable and because their refined colours were mixed in garments that were considered daring. They revolutionized style as well as production in the decades to come.

In France, Sonia Rykiel was considered a pioneer of this style. In 1971, the brand created by the Benetton brothers, who would open their franchise in cities throughout the world, emerged on the international scene. With a forward-looking approach and entrepreneurial spirit, instead of using wool in diverse colours in the production of knitwear, they created several models using recycled raw wool that was "dyed on the garment", depending on the requirements of the moment, so as to be able to replenish their stores at a faster pace. The Benetton group also owed its popularity to an innovative communication style that informed the public about social issues, an initiative developed by Fabrica, Benetton's communications research centre. Supporting a nonconformist look, the passion for fanciful knitwear continued in wrap dresses with a V-neck that tied at the waist and were fitted on the hips, the creation launched onto the market by designer Diane von Furstenberg in the first years of the decade. A more free expression of the comfort-chic concept, both for work and leisure, combined with tight knee-high boots it became the quintessential day attire and all department stores had their own versions in all sizes, as the fluid lines of the dress finally allowed women to be themselves.

Prêt-à-porter fashion shows in Paris dropped the traditional presentation of the ateliers and turned into spectacular shows.

Lancetti, *Russian Look*, 1974-1975

THE FIORUCCI PHENOMENON

In Italy, Elio Fiorucci was one of the first to advance a form of fashion that went against the tide, taking the initial steps in this direction with a small family business. In a few years, he created a large emporium-bazaar in Milan characterised by a unique atmosphere and frequented primarily by very young men. Actor Adrian Celentano, who went to the event riding a pink Cadillac, inaugurated his first business, in Galleria Passarella, in 1967. There one could find new and fun articles imported from England and the United States. One could listen to music, smell sandalwood and incense fragrances and have a multi-sensory experience with an edge of transgression. While the business still did not use the concept of "lifestyle", Fiorucci brought together in a single space, oriental garments, printed t-shirts, faded jeans and all types of accessories (costume jewellery, plastic bags, sweatshirts, little decorative objects and colourful gadgets). Encouraged by his success, Fiorucci opened stores in New York, London, Los Angeles, Paris and other European cities.

Walter Albini and his team, 1970

Drawing by Walter Albini

The maxi garments had giant fantasy surfaces, made of large stylized elements that looked as if they expanded inside each other to the rhythm of fireworks, inspired on the one hand, by pop-art and psychedelia and on the other, by the revival of turn of the century graphic arts. Fascination with the east was apparent, from India to Afghanistan and from Morocco to Turkey. The export of trinkets provided stylists with new details for fabrics used in boutique garments for sophisticated women, including from shirt-dresses and night attire. The divine Saint Laurent also turned to folklore when creating a sumptuous collection of Russian style and a subsequent one inspired by China.

The rhythm of renovation in fashion became accelerated. In the early 1970s, a new generation of designers that would decisively influence the styles of the decade to come made their debut: Jean-Charles de Castelbajac, Claude Montana and Jean Paul Gaultier. At the same time, Paris opens the doors to Japanese creativity: Kenzo, Rei Kawakubo, founder of the brand Comme des Garçons in 1973, Issey Miyake, Hanae Mori and Yohji Yamamoto.

The "textile chain" model was defined, a organizational structure made of many smaller specialized companies, each with a specific role, that participate to varying degrees in some of the stages of the industrial production process. The strong synergies between fashion design and industry, with Milan as the epicentre, defined a significant turn in the history of Italian fashion, catapulting this city onto the international scene. In the 1980's, the "Made in Italy" label became an international fixture.

Diane von Furstenberg, 1974

Women with long skirts and V-necks, 1975

Pierre Balmaine, 1970

Christian Dior, 1971

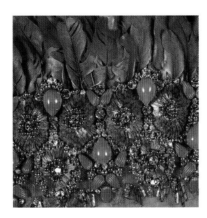

Scene from the movie Love story

PUNK FASHION

The punk movement, born in 1976, represented a decisive break with the past in the name of an avant-garde that cast itself out voluntarily into the margins of society. Until then, the term "punk" was used in a derogative way to designate swindlers and criminals. Around 1975, however, punk represented the music of Patti Smith, guitar player Lenny Kaye and Bruce Springsteen, who layered a fast, aggressive, distorted sound over a rock and roll foundation. Punk became a fashion phenomenon thanks to Vivienne Westwood, Malcolm McLaren's

partner, the *enfant terrible* of the Sex Pistols. Together they opened, in 1974, a small store that popularized the taste for black leather fetish garments accessorized with chains, padlocks, safety pins, metal rivets and piercings. Soon a line of single size (S/M) attire was born, defined by their creators as "rubber rags for work". The style materialized with the slogans "Fuck Off" and "No Future" printed on ripped t-shirts with holes and cuts that symbolized the interior rage of more than one generation. Bodies were plastered with gaudy tattoos; the hair, shaved on the side, arose in a crest dyed fluorescent green or blue, a hairdo similar to that of Iroquois warriors. Vivienne Westwood became the preferred designer of the counterculture. Because of her eccentricity and irreverence, however, her creations also appeared on international fashion runways, reinterpreting classic British themes in an ironic and cheeky tone.

Typical punk attire of the 1970's

DAVID BOWIE AND GLAM ROCK

David Bowie achieved fame during the first half of the 1970's. His album *Ziggy Stardust* came out in 1972, a little after Apollo XI (1969) landed on the moon. On his tours, he created a futuristic atmosphere that mixed science fiction and cartoons and wore androgynous outfits, distinctive and flashy makeup, feathers, sequins and exaggerated hats, adopting feminine and sexually ambiguous behaviours. His style, as well as that of Roxy Music (and before that, Marc Bolan and T.Rex, though in a lighter and more superficial way), was based above all on image. At the same time, Bowie introduced an introspective artistic

and experimental element that was not opposed to a romantic melody. There were several *glam rock* bands in the United States as well, such as Alice Cooper and Iggy Pop, who in his concerts made explicit allusions of sexual nature. These manifestations of glam rock could be violent and macabre, driven by a spirit so ironic and offensive that this type of music came to be called "shock rock". Glam exerted a great deal of influence on many young people at the time, who would later become the face of British punk, and was also important for the birth in the 1980's of pop metal, a commercial version of heavy metal.

FASHION IN THE 1980s

The hedonism of the Reagan years defined a markedly individu-alistic trend that was adopted by Western society in the decade of the 1980s. The election of Ronald Reagan as president of the United States in 1979 inaugurated a conservative era, reinforced in Europe by the ascent to power of Margaret Thatcher, the Iron Lady of Britain.

Luxury was expressed through the possession of superfluous things, the exclusivity of brand-name products and ostentatious exhibition of expensive design objects. In the United States, the yuppie phenomenon emerged ("yuppie" is an acronym for Young Urban Professional). An ambitious upstart, the typical yuppie worked in the stock market, lacked scruples and was looking for a quick way to get rich. Yuppies frequented chic circles and exclu-sive restaurants, consumed cocaine and wore clothes by Italian designers such as Armani and Versace.

The movie *American Gigolo* starring Richard Gere, one of the most desired men in Hollywood, was a meaningful portrait of the prevailing cultural climate in those days. In line with these values, the style in clothing was characterized by a cult of efficiency and "dressing for success". The preference for "Made in Italy" articles was the product of skillful and calculated marketing strategies: the eagle became Armani's emblem; Krizia chose the panther; the greyhound represented Trussardi; and Medusa was the characteristic logo of Versace. Fascination with prominent brands grew expo-nentially and their dominance could be felt in everything related to clothing, while the market for Italian style fashion became more international. This was the decade of sexual provocation and post-feminist spirit for the career woman, no longer fragile or feminine but self-confident and tough, projecting her image

THE FASHION OF GIORGIO ARMANI

Armani, 1980

After working as a purchasing assistant for the department store La Rinascente, Giorgio Armani went to work for Cerruti's Hitman. In 1978, with Gruppo Finanziario Tessile, he began a new form of collaboration with the industry based on production contracts under license, creating casual wear, knitwear, shirts, ties, umbrellas, trousers, leather goods, jeans and perfumes. A baby-clothes line and a household goods line soon followed. When Richard Gere opened his well-apportioned closet in *American Gigolo* and arranged a series of combinations of Armani shirts, ties and jackets on the bed in order to be able to choose the most striking outfit, everyone knew for a fact that masculine seduction par excellence could not be defined in any other way. The fashion designer even coined a name for a new colour: *greige*, a very light pearl grey between grey and beige. The fabrics were tightly woven with dyed fine-fibre thread, pure or mixed with viscose, which provided fluidity and hang, and the finishes were soft to the touch. The garments, according to Armani, should have an air of having been worn, adapting to the body with a relaxed seduction corresponding to new social manners. The notion of the soft suit thus prevailed, preferred above all by young people eager to assert themselves in the world with style and dynamism, leaving behind a strict and stiff tradition that was already obsolete. While Missoni proposed comfortable, colourful sweaters with sophisticated geometric motifs inspired by the palette of the Impressionists and combined with leather jackets and Loden coats, king Giorgio became the spokesperson of the new "Made in Italy", which would land him on the 5 April 1982 cover of Time magazine.

into the realm of work. Giorgio Armani was the designer that best interpreted that image, devoting his collections to the deconstruction of the men's blazer without lining or inside reinforcements (except for the shoulder pads, which, in time, would become even larger) and recreating a more comfortable and elegant version to satisfy the new feminine requirements.

For the "executive woman", well-trained and prepared, the suit and blazer's shoulders became wider, and the outfit was completed with a small pencil skirt – the waist marked with an elastic waistband – which sometimes was substituted by wide, wool Bermuda shorts. Shoes had medium heels and the handbag became a practical briefcase with a strap to carry it on the shoulder. Women also wore fitted trousers with pumps with the blazer. The functionality of the garments for both men and women was of the highest importance. The hang of the fabric facilitated more dynamic movement. At night, the style was more ostentatious. Garments were Hollywood inspired, accessorized with showy jewelry, distinct makeup and frizzy hair very similar to the hairdos of Linda Gray and Joan Collins in series such as *Dallas* (1978-1991) and *Dynasty* (1981-1991) where sex, money, lies and all sorts of intrigue reigned. Sequined garments were a hit. Parisian embroiderer François Lesage fashioned exclusive embroideries inspired by Van Gogh's lilies and sunflowers for Yves Saint Laurent's blazers. The countless string of TV shows offered interesting looks into the private lives of the upper class and the excessive tastes of its members. Men's fashion, while retaining the "high finance" style represented by the German brand Hugo Boss, Hugo Boss, adopted softer features, as seen in the television series Miami Vice, an "MTV-style" story of two Miami policeman set within an atmosphere of glamour and synthesizer music, a significant element of the action's narrative. Trendily dressed in labeled suits, the policemen drove around Miami in a white Ferrari Testarossa. They wore pastel-coloured outfits that matched the décor of the room they were in and sported Ray-Bans, in the process defining the masculine image of the 1980s. The tear-shaped Aviator sunglasses, combined with a leather jacket, appeared in another cult movie, *Top Gun*, starring Tom Cruise.

Yves Saint Laurent, 1980

Antonio López para Missoni, 1984

The profession of the designer was modernized, redefined primarily as a male-oriented figure capable of using sophisticated media campaigns to reach the desired target and successfully consolidate the designer's own image. They included Gianni Versace, Krizia, Rosita and Ottavio Missoni, Nicola Trussardi, Franco Moschino, Gianfranco Ferré, Alberta Ferretti and Blumarine, to name just a few. The euphoria of those years in a city filled with unprecedented optimism and frenzy, countless work-related appointments and social encounters, boutique inaugurations, dinners, awards, concerts, parties and fashion *vernissages* was palpable. Each designer knew how to intelligently develop the personality cult of the creator: a sophisticated aesthete in all senses, master of taste and constructor of style, skillful with pencil and scissors, adjusting a detail in a single glance, enhancing a pleat, embellishing a collar, adding a ribbon or repositioning something on the garment. The advent of the computer introduced new production technologies to fashion. Garments were designed with the help of CAD/CAM software, which made the rapid reproduction of shapes, models, signs, textures, fabrics and color variations possible. For this reason, the costume designer profession disappeared. A computer was used to create the pattern of the garment and develop its sizes, in order to transfer the data directly to the proper place on the fabric. The increased precision of the technique led to savings in the costs of raw material and accelerated the turnaround time of the merchandise.

Once the importance of French haute couture was cut back, prêt-à-porter flourished. The creations of Claude Montana stood out. Specializing in leatherwear, he created jackets with enormous enveloping collars that closed with a single button. Also noteworthy was the work of Thierry Mugler, who preferred the theatrical effect of latex and vinyl, exaggerated shoulder pads and runways with futuristic staging. The cartoon-like creations of Jean Charles de Castelbajac transcended the seasonal whims of fashion while the designs of Karl Lagerfeld, the highly disciplined German designer who, in 1983, became Chanel's creative director, were also highly appreciated. Christian Lacroix, who opulently united baroque influences and folklore inspired by a type of woman characterised

Missoni, 1988

Sarli, Roma, 1980

by vibrant colors and extravagant accessories, gained prominence. At the same time, Jean Paul Gaultier, influenced by the cinematic atmospheres of filmmaker Rainer Werner Fassbinder, replete with strong sailors and muscular uniformed army men, ingeniously embraced with conviction the prevailing androgynous style, transcending gender differences. Gaultier dressed men in beach wraps and kilts on the fashion runway, and women appeared in tuxedos, proposals that recurred in many of his collections. Celebrities such as Prince and Boy George contributed to a large extent to the transformation of men's identity. Boy George, leader of the band Culture Club, experimented continuously with surprising discoveries. The front man did not hesitate to wear, say, an embroidered nightgown, a hat and African tresses like the ones worn by Bo Derek, an international erotic icon who emerged on the scene in 1979 in the movie *10* by Blake Edwards.

The music channel MTV made its debut in the life of teenagers and developed an inclination for pop culture that revolutionized the way music was consumed. Designers and particular brands began to associate with specific artists. Creating outfits for pop stars was a way to make oneself known. Antony Price was considered to be the initiator of this phenomenon. Since the 1970's, he had designed the fitted garments of Bryan Ferry. In the video of his successful song "Faith", George Michael wore a biker's jacket with the words "Rockers Revenge" emblazoned on the back. The early Madonna of "Material Girl" dressed in suburban attire. She had curly blonde hair with visible black roots parted on the side and held up with ribbons and bows. Her lips were painted purple and she wore a lot

Benetton advertisement, 1985

From Vogue, 1988, wool and silk;
© Setarium, Silk Museum of Como, Italy

DONOVAN

© Setarium, 1989

© Setarium, 1988

of makeup, along with short skirts combined with leggings and ankle boots, lace fingerless gloves, necklaces with crosses and plastic bracelets. In a short period of time, she became the idol of teenage girls, who copied her look as well as her feisty irreverent attitude.

In England, Vivienne Westwood drew inspiration from the past. In 1981, she launched a collection named "Pirate" that popularized the new "romantic" look, with shirts with flounces and lace frills, velvet jackets, capes and phantasy hats. Spandau Ballet, David Bowie, Visage and Duran Duran, whose image was managed by Perry Haines, incorporated these garments into their costumes. The brilliant designer soon created another collection, "Nostalgia of Mud", which recreated the retro-futuristic attire of the replicants in the movie *Blade Runner* (1982). In 1984, Katharine Hamnet launched the line "Choose Life", consisting of a collection of t-shirts with printed sentences that encouraged world peace and "No Nukes" and was devoted to protecting the environment. The general picture was completed with the subversive trends of post-punk and other urban youth cultures of Afro-American, Caribbean or Latin orgin: primarily rap and hip-hop. The purveyors of these movements wore bomber jackets, baseball hats and wide, comfortable "home-boy style" clothing and invented the syncopated movements of breakdancing. Alongside these trends was the influence of emerging Japanese designers, who had immigrated to Paris and preferred little known materials and asymmetric lines and impeccable cuts.

Valentino, 1988, embroidery by Pino Grasso

In the collective imagination, the eighties represented a wild form of narcissism taken to extremes and a true obsession with fashion. Inspiration was sought everywhere. Numerous unusual styles were created that followed American trends that had emerged from the first cinema special effects and computerized graphics shown on television. In Italy, the trend on the street emulated to the unbridled American consumerism as well. The *paninari*, or well-off youths from Milan, gathered at the country's first fast-food establishments and dressed in Best Company sweaters, Moncler padded jackets, Timberland boots and rolled-up jeans. The red leather suit Michael Jackson wore in the video *Thriller*, white socks with loafers, Nike, Adidas and Puma running shoes and the sweater tucked into the trousers were styles that resulted from the emerging hip-hop culture. Even not so young people wore garments inspired by sports attire. The "causal" style was universally predominant, equalizing social classes and becoming an authentic revolution. Jeans reigned supreme while all the acclaimed designers created secondary brands at more affordable prices that included branded jeans and leatherwear. Women were fully emancipated and devoted themselves to the cult of their own bodies. The benefits of jogging were visible. People could be seen running vigorously in city parks wearing a gym bodysuit, Walkman and headphones and a fanny pack for their personal belongings.

JAPANESE DESIGNERS

Issey Miyake – Styliste japonais

The most colouristic of the Japanese creators, Kenzo constitutes a special case. He combined the Japanese capacity for synthesizing with Mexican, Norwegian, and oriental folklore elements in a hotchpotch of always captivating designs that anticipated a contemporary globe-trotter style. Yssey Miyake, who rejected the prejudices toward synthetic fibers, became the new exponent of pleated fabric that explored all possible variations, infusing Western fashion with new ideas regarding experimentation with the material, which became predominant in the definition of the shape of the garments. Hanae Mori opened her atelier in 1951 and initially worked as wardrobe designer on hundreds of movies. After a period in the sixties when she was in New York, she returned to Paris where she quickly proved that she had assimilated the concept of elegant and very feminine fashion with a Western character. She developed drapes with her ethereal silks and drew inspiration from butterflies for drawings. Rei Kawakubo founded the brand Comme des Garçons in 1973 and devoted herself to the asymmetric deconstruction of shapes, reconstructing them with cuts, fillings, drapes and superimpositions that hide the figure underneath. Inclined toward the styles of "survivors of nuclear disaster", she introduced tears and lacerations on austere shapes that embodied the anti-fashion concept, combined with total black, white and neutral grays. Yohji Yamamoto was a believer in an ascetic and rigorous line. She created sculpted but fluid silhouettes with bias cuts and black stratifications that tended to create room for movement around the body. She proposed an almost identical look for men and women, with a marked inclination toward urban casual that reflected a refusal to adapt to the reigning seasonal rules. Yohji Yamamoto and Rei Kawakubo introduced on fashion runways black Doc Martens, robust black leather boots with rubber soles that tied with laces that pass through holes and lateral safety strips that had been adopted by punk youths.

TOP MODELS

Advertising photographers, working closely with casting agencies, emphasized the image of the top model, a term coined in those years to describe an unattainable woman with a perfect physique that dominated the collective consciousness and constituted the period's ideal of beauty. Among the best-known faces in fashion magazines and on cosmetic brands was the precocious Brooke Shields, a model since childhood chosen to be the protagonist of a Calvin Klein jeans' advertisement. Well-known is the sentence: "What comes between me and my Calvins? Nothing." Other famous models were Inès de la Fressange, under exclusive contract to Chanel, who was Karl Lagerfeld's muse; Iman, the dark-skinned model of choice of Gianni Versace; Cindy Crawford, with her distinctive beauty mark alongside her mouth; Yasmin Le Bon, wife of Simon Le Bon, leader of Duran Duran; Elle Macpherson, known as "The Body" because of her measurements; Paulina Porizkova, who, in 1983, appeared in a documentary about fashion entitled *Portfolio*; Carol Alt, who appeared on more than 500 covers and became one of the most famous models of her generation. The most popular photographers were Richard Avedon, Irving Penn, Bruce Weber, Gian Paolo Barbieri and Lou Castel.

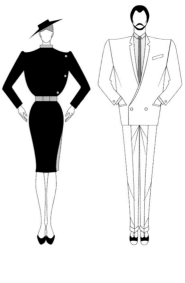

Krizia, 1988

Benneton advertisement, 1985

Antonio López and Karl Lagerfeld for Chloé,
1983

Chanel, 1984

20th Century

Men and women devoted many exhausting hours to bodybuilding at the gym. Thanks in part to Jane Fonda, the actress who had become an aerobics instructor, the search for the sculpted body became an obsession. Alongside the Levi's 501 jeans worn by Marty McFly in *Back to the Future*, appeared Lycra body suits in fluorescent colors, leggings combined with white t-shirts with bat-wing sleeves that revealed one shoulder, cycling shorts and tight tops, leg-warmers and towel head-bands for a "dancing school" style that movies such as *Flashdance* and *Fame* contributed to popularizing. Shiny fabrics and intense colours replaced the mandatory dress code of the past. Singer Tina Turner preferred Azzedine Alaïa's wrapping dresses, which did not add a single superfluous millimeter to the shape of the body, such as the ones worn by the women in Robert Palmer's video "Addicted to Love" (1985). In line with "minimal body art", Alaïa, a French designer of Tunisian origin, proposed short knit garments that adhered to the body with spiral seams and zippers in strategic locations. He designed Lycra leggings that defined the silhouette. Thanks to these, he received the name "King of the Kling". The dual benefit of Lycra, mixed with fibers such as cotton or wool, provided greater freedom of movement and at the same time allowed for exhibiting and emphasizing the body. On beaches filled with suntanned bodies thanks to hours and hours of exposure to UV rays on tanning beds or new self-tanning cosmetics, women wore minimal clothing. Men wore the new boxer style bathing suits. Used as underwear, they began to appear in the United States, under the Calvin Klein brand.

The profession of the model, a woman celebrated as the new Venus, capable of drawing attention to the most prestigious brands, who works for advertising agencies and fashion houses, became extremely profitable. Models began to be paid very high daily fees. Hired not just for fashion runways but mainly special guests in the advertising campaigns of multinational companies in the beauty industry, the top models travelled around the world and became stars, important figures thanks to garments designers' creations.

FILMS

10 (1979), Blake Edwards

American Gigol (1980), Paul Schrader.

Blade Runner (1982), Ridley Scott.

Nothing Underneath (1985), Carlo Vanzina

Yuppies, i giovani di successo (1986), Carlo Vanzina

Via Montenapoleone (1987), Carlo Vanzina

Miami Vice, American crime series, created by Anthony Yerkovich and produced between 1984 and 1989

Top Gun (1986), Tony Scott

Dynasty (1981-91), Richard and Esther Shapiro

Back to the Future (1985), Robert Zemeckis

Flashdance (1983), Adrian Lybe

Fame (1980), Alan Parker

Who's That Girl (1987), James Foley

Desperately Seeking Susan (1985), Susan Seidelman

Notebook on Cities and Clothes (1989), Wim Wenders

Mannequin (1987), Michael Gottlieb

Flashdance, 1985

Regreso al futuro, 1985

Tina Turner, 1990

FASHION IN THE 1990s

In 1991, Tim Berners-Lee invented the World Wide Web and from then on, the world began to "surf". Suddenly, conditions for sharing ideas and information were created that facilitated the globalisation of markets. Individual states distanced themselves somewhat from their internal problems and approached international events with more interest. With the fall of the Berlin Wall in 1989, many political, social and existential barriers also crumbled. In parallel, the world of fashion expanded, including French, Italian, British, American and Japanese designers who continued exercising an irresistible attraction on fashion runways, which were increasingly spectacular. The objective of fashion was to transmit an identity, impose a style and disseminate the culture of brands through communication. At the same time, everything from "below", what could be acquired in stores in alternative in neighbourhoods or appeared in music magazines, on albums, in video clips, on television and in the movies quickly became fashionable.

In 1990, the Stedelijk Museum in Amsterdam organized the exhibition "Energies", which demonstrated the meaningful relationships between the different artistic disciplines: architecture, drawing, painting, sculpture, video, theatre and fashion, uncovering analogies and differences in the manufacturing of structures. The world in the early days of the Internet seemed to herald the end of ideologies and certainties and was centred around the elaboration of a network of meanings, a hotchpotch

Versace, 1991

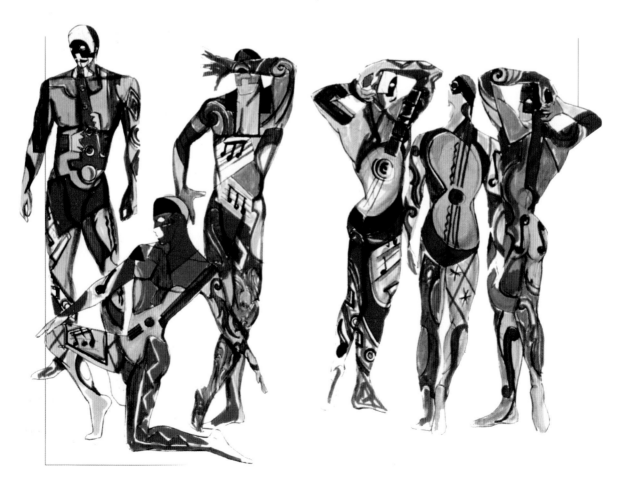

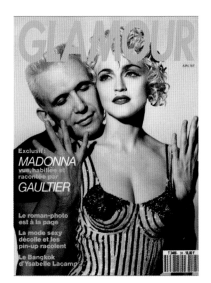

Cover of *Glamour* with Madonna and Jean Paul Gaultier, 1990

Manu Brambatti: Jean Paul Gaultier for Madonna's *Blond Ambition Tour*, 1990

of knowledge that was exciting and disorienting at the same time. Interdependent and isolated ideas combined, buttressing the new passion for technology or nostalgia for the past. In fashion, this concept would be expressed in an unequivocal trend. Yet, it would also create an aesthetic mix, one in a precarious balance between subtlety and provocation, which associated casual fashion and formal attire, creating hybrids in terms of style. The Palais Galierà, a fashion and dress museum in Paris, paraphrasing the immense power of fashion over the collective imagination, organized the exhibition "Le monde selon ses createurs" ("The World According to its Creators"), grouping together six designers: Jean Paul Gautier, Romeo Gigli, Vivienne Westwood, Sybilla, Martin Margiela and Jean-Charles de Castelbajac, emblematic examples of a dynamic creative sensibility keen on capturing the spirit of the times but also aware of the historical references of their inspiration.

The *enfant terrible* Jean Paul Gautier, devoted to provocation and the establishment of "queer culture" (a theory that questioned the notion that gender is biological) within the panorama of fashion, created the famous cone-shaped corset that Madonna wore on her Blond Ambition Tour, in 1990. The American singer also asked him to design the garments for her Confessions Tour, in 2006. Romeo Gigli, who defined himself as "not a stylist, not an artist, but a designer who came to fashion by accident", was a visionary. Travel was his source of inspiration. Each collection was replete with powerful influxes of dream imagery and high-brow references: from Byzantium to Africa, from Zen Buddhism to languid pre-Raphaelite women. His most emblematic garments are the colour of spices and have a cocoon silhouette that respects the body: shirts with interminable sleeves on top of which miniscule crossed tops or short boleros are superimposed; large sarong skirts; deconstructed jackets with high buttons and wraparound coats with descending shoulders.

Vivienne Westwood, the eccentric designer with a fire-red mane of hair, capable of transforming any aspect of urban subculture into fashion, is today considered a star of the fashion runway. In the 90s, continuing her struggle against the conventionalism and mediocrity of everyday life, she sought to provoke the public in a cultivated and fun way, updating court dresses from the past. In the name of individuality, she recreated mini crinolines and English tartans, reinforced bustier and Elizabethan ruffs, complementing them with ankle boots, very high pointy platform shoes with rivets and flats with rocking-chair soles that knotted at the ankle.

The Spanish designer Sybilla appeared in 1986 with an ironic style, a fairy-tale modernity that was graphically appealing. Her creations were presented on international fashion runways and achieved wide popularity in Japan, where they connected with adolescent tastes. In 1996, she designed and marketed a line for the home, followed in 1998 by a nightwear line and a bridal line. Martin Margiela was one of the promoters of frayed selvedge, of apparently unfinished garments, deconstructed and reconstructed couture using a combination of traditionally incompatible fabrics and materials. In reference to these structural characteristics of the creative process, the specialised press spoke of the "de-contraction" of fashion. In the 90s, Jean-Charles de Castelbajac became famous for the exuberance of colour contrasts, gigantic graphic elements, the efficiency of pop language and references to the world of comic books. His interminable string of successful achievements is crowned by the immediacy of the image and a passion for graffiti and street art. At the beginning of the decade, Mikhail Gorbachev received the Nobel Peace Prize and news of the release of Nelson Mandela revitalized the hope for the attainment of civil rights for African people. In response to the illusion that a wealthy and tumultuous society, based on entrenched social inequalities, could ensure peace and happiness for everyone, in addition to the emergence of the AIDS epidemic, which had begun to kill its victims, the "new age" phenomenon emerged. This was a current of thought dedicated to introspection and seriousness, one that promoted a return to health and nature and a more relaxed and less competitive pace of life. The opportunity to benefit from scientific progress offered an already privatised body the temptation, increasingly frequent, to resort to cosmetic surgery, inverting the old motto *mens sana in corpore sano*. The innovating airs of the new age introduced in fashion an aesthetic minimalism, foreshadowed by the monastic proposals of Japanese purists, who were concerned with the experimental search for form, material and space.

As an alternative to the glitter and excess of hyper-ornamented luxury and the kitsch exaggerations of the 80s, a new manner of thinking about design emerged: a liberating act that does not exclude invention and fantasy but synthesises them. Conceptual garments, monochromatic by nature, that spoke the language of a genuine avant-garde product, appeared.

Reconnecting with modern style, the severity of the minimalist style of the 90s exalted formal purity and pushed fashion progressively into a continuous dialogue with adjacent disciplines: plastic arts,

Gianfranco Ferré, model and drawing, A/W 1994-95

Missoni, 1990

TATTOO FASHION

In his 1994 S/S collection, Jean Paul Gaultier introduced to the catwalks models with real tattoos that were in harmony with the prints on the chiffon fabrics of the garments. Avant-garde fashion officialised these body practices which in the past had been associated with problematic people and enshrined the art of the tattoo as one of the new accessories in vogue in the fashion system. Permanent tattoos also appeared on the face to redefine the outlines of the lips, eyes and eyebrows, ensuring that the makeup is always perfect. The punk movement had already imprinted messages and emblems with renewed meanings in "acts of senseless beauty" through piercings and tattoos that were imposed as destabilising signs in an indifferent society accustomed to everything. In 1995, the first perfume for men, *Le Mâle* by Jean Paul Gaultier, appeared. Enclosed in an opaque blue bottle that reproduced a male bust without arms and head, the torso was covered in clear horizontal bands in imitation of a sailor's shirt. The different versions of the fragrance, which appeared from 1999 to 2007, made reference to the art of the tattoo in the selection of the packaging and in the choice of the models, always muscular and heavily tattooed, for the advertising campaigns.

"LE MALE" *par Jean Paul Gaultier*

architecture and photography, obtaining surprising results through the balance between formal abstraction and concrete functionality. The most eloquent exponent of this trend was the Austrian Helmut Lang, with his simple silhouettes, defined impeccable cuts, "raw-cut" stitching and techno-fibres used in bright-opaque combination or glazed on naked skin. It was a modern urban style that would be widely copied and that inaugurated the use of basic garments with very limited colours and adornments. It was also innovative in the presentation of the product, transforming the runway into a place of performance. Turkish designer Rifat Ozbek, who in 1989 received the British Fashion Award, experimented with video as an alternative to catwalk processions.

Contemporary luxury, now based on the concept of "less is more" of Mies van der Rohe, acquired new connotations of rigour and cleanliness, values shared by the designs of Jil Sander in the form of practical garments that rest on the body and thanks to which, all types of attire tended to become simplified: pants suit, blazers and straight-line skirts and simple sweaters in neutral and sober colours. To total black, spurred by the different textile consistencies, were added sophisticated combinations of black and blue, black and brown, white and flesh tone. The minimalist trend, enhanced by the black-and-white images of photographer Peter Lindbergh, descended upon Milanese catwalks, considered the privileged place of good taste and wearable garments, contributing to the consolidation of the creations of American designers Calvin Klein and Donna Karan, aimed at the cosmopolitan style of the Big Apple. America designer Tom Ford assumed creative direction of the Italian brand Gucci and imprinted a radical renovation on the company, which returned to prominence after a long crisis in the 70s and 80s. Traditional and formal dress experienced a further push with the arrival of the Antwerp Six, a group of graduate students in the Royal Academy of Fine Arts who presented their collections jointly in London.

Manu Brambatti for Versace, 1991

Martin Margiela, 1998

Gianfranco Ferrè, 1995, embroidery Pino Grasso

The young protagonists of Belgian fashion quickly became known on the international scene. Ann Demeulemeester, creator of a sensually androgynous style, worked in achromatic black and white tones with some touches of red. Sensitive to disparate influences, from Gothic to punk, she designed garments rich in interior suggestions that had to communicate all of their poetry through touch. In 1998, she dismembered her garments in parts and put written notes in the sleeves to facilitate re-composition. Martin Margiela played ironically with the desire to pretend, subverting the concept garment by transferring the stitches, lining and labels to the outside; he promoted the cult of the impersonality of the designer, ultimately substituting the creator's name with blank labels or the numbers 0 to 23 enclosed in circles. From 1997 to 2002 he was creative director of Hermès. Dries van Noten designed sartorially influential garments that conquered an elitist public. He constructed his designs by joining refined fabrics and rustic cloths and stylizing graphic designs of diverse origin, which he intellectualised by adding them to stylish formal classic jackets. He used earthy colours, which he ironically placed alongside bright tones and a mix of prints of floral and ethnic inspiration. Dirk Bikkembergs designed men and women's collections, moving from the rigorous and stylised masculine style to the use of Lurex and tight corsets. His creations became very popular among young people after the launch of the line "Bikkembergs Sport" and a line of shoes for which he has been known since 1986. Walter van Beirendonck creates very ironic collections inspired by visual arts, comic books and literature, with unusual colour combinations and updated ethnic influences and has his own brand, W&LT, Wild Lethal Trash. Since 1992, he has collaborated with Gianfranco Ferré on the sports garments line Rhinosaurus Rex. In 1997 he designed the wardrobe for U2's Popmart tour, and in 1998, the uniform for the cyclists in the Belgian Tour. For twelve years, from 1984 to 1996, he was a

LARA CROFT: THE VIRTUAL WOMAN

With the rapid spread of digital technology, in 1995 the fictional character Lara Croft, a virtual archaeologist of affluent means and heroine of the video series *Tomb Raider*, was created. To interact with her and engage passionately in her adventures throughout the world, a PC or PlayStation console was necessary. Her captivating appearance, characterised by a long braid and her presence as a powerful woman who demonstrates extraordinary athletic skills, quickly transformed Lara Croft into one of the idols of the time. In 1998 she was chosen as one of the sexiest women of the year.

Endowed also with exceptional reflexes that allow her to handle herself successfully in hand-to-hand combat with knives or firearms, Lara wears a sea green Lyrca top, shorts with a belt, fingerless leather gloves and mid-calf-length boots. She is an expert in technology and is armed with two pistols sheathed in holsters, attached to her thighs with a leather band. Many fashion collections were inspired by her image, ever since U2 choose her for one of their videos and girls began to want to imitate her style. Movies and comic books based on the virtual Lara Croft followed.

professor at the Royal Academy of Fine Arts in Antwerp, a quarry of fashion talents. Currently he sells his creations on line as well.

Cherished brands and designers, aware at that time of the sociocultural scope of dress style, did not live isolated in their ivory towers. Instead they travelled continuously, immersing themselves in the street. On any accessible corner of the globe, enthusiastic young assistants, endowed with a particular sensibility, interacted with ordinary people, observing in squares and street markets, stores and places of worship, bookstores and boutiques, monitoring the market in search of creative trends to appropriate. New professionals emerged: trend makers, trendsetters, cool-hunters, image consultants, etc., dedicated to observing the tastes and preferences of small segments of customers and engaged in the search for emerging signs, preferences capable of serving as a catalyst, determining and even deducing a new fashion trend.

At that time fashion constituted a creative plus in consumer society, subject to rapid obsolescence. To renew itself on an international scale each season, designers needed to have at their disposal people that interacted with the outside world and captured ideas from among dreams and desires or everyday life. The technological reproduction of images hastened assimilation and the creation of a virtual reality and parallel collective imagination that generated confusion vis-a-vis the perceived reality. In any event, beyond the latest trends there was always youth culture. In fact, fashion magazines refused to suggest a single overarching model and began to give prominence to diverse trends, often very different from each other: grunge and hip hop, already fashionable in the 80s, or Goth style and rave, leaving the public a great deal of freedom to customise its appearance.

Western society was literally bombarded with advertising, which, in the name of the free market and the desire to beat the competition, became even more intrusive and influential. In 1996, McDonald's, the largest fast-food chain in the world, signed an agreement to develop the rights of Walt Disney characters, which proved strategic for the marketing campaign directed at the youngest consumers. The top models gracing the catwalks were Christy

Manu Brambatti for Versace, 1998

Turlington, Naomi Campbell, Linda Evangelista, Eva Herzigova, Tatjana Patitz, Stephanie Seymour, Cindy Crawford and Carla Bruni. Their beauty, compensated with fees worthy of Hollywood, exalted the same aesthetic canons of fashion and its consumers. Boyish women with less characteristic faces and who were increasingly younger would replace them.

Fashion models were no longer mannequins but versatile women independent of the simple catwalk. They preferred young emerging designers in search of new styles, less glamorous and more minimalist. Paris retained its excellent reputation in fashion presentations, which always guarantees high visibility. However, maintaining the onerous costs of haute couture became unsustainable, especially after the general decline in the consumption of luxury goods and the massive expansion of prêt-à-porter at the international level. Exclusive French organisations pondered the possible strategies for balancing these large losses and renovating their image. They opted for a series of generational handovers that led to the hiring of young British talent with which they entrusted the artistic direction of some of the most important fashion houses: John Galliano became the artistic director of Givenchy and later Christian Dior; Alexander McQueen succeeded him at Givenchy, and Stella McCartney has collaborated with Chloe since 1997. The production system on which the broad success of "Made in Italy"

GRUNGE FASHION

Grunge was born in Seattle, a city in the mid 1980s, affected by poverty, unemployment and a high rate of heroin use. Grunge music groups – the term grunge means "grimy" – denounced the political and cultural system at the time. They distanced themselves from pure rock and looked towards the "Seattle sound", a very local musical genre that included Nirvana, Pearl Jam, Soundgarden and Alice in Chains, The young musicians were distinguished by their long, dishevelled hair, loose ragged t-shirts with images or messages emblazoned on them, jeans split at the knees, old Converse sneakers, deformed sweaters and plaid flannel shirts typical of local lumberjacks, which they wore unbuttoned. Their dirty look, somewhere between hippy and punk, connected with fans that identified with the generalised social discontent and adopted the dress style of Kurt Cobain, leader of Nirvana, who committed suicide in 1994, and his wife Courtney Love, who played in the group Hole. The feminine version of grunge is the *dessous look*, consisting of intentionally torn red stockings worn with black military boots, wrinkled combinations, loose short minidresses, miniskirts and withered silk tops, combined with handmade pullovers and heavy coats. A product of the suburban streets, it was not long before grunge appeared on fashion runways, thanks to Anna Sui, Marc Jacobs, Cristian Lacroix, Donna Karan and Karl Lagerfeld, influencing fashion far more dramatically than the purely musical phenomenon. The typical female grunge look was hollow-eyed with makeup running on a pale and haggard face, an absent gaze and a drugged expression. The models were bony and angular, skinny to the point of being anorexic. All of this inspired the "heroin chic" trend, a symbol of the period, predominant in the photographic work of Davide Sorrenti, identifiable with what the *Los Angeles Times* defined, in 1996, as a "nihilistic vision of beauty". More commercial photographers began to copy this glamorous romanticising of drug addiction, using models such as Kate Moss and Vincent Gallo, the protagonists of a campaign for Calvin Klein.

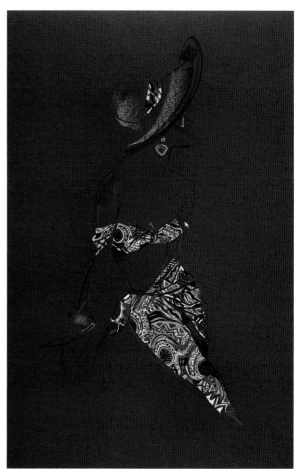

THE SPICE GIRLS

The pop group the Spice Girls burst onto the scene in London, gaining wide commercial and artistic success with the single "Wannabe", which reached the top of the list of British hits in 1996. The band, considered the most successful female group of all time, consisted of Geri Halliwell, Melanie C, Victoria Adams, Melanie B and Emma Bunton, tapped into the collective unconscious, offering their visages to clever merchandising operations with Pepsi, Polaroid, Sony and other important brands. In 1997, *Spiceworld: The Movie*, directed by Bob Spiers, in which the five girls humorously played themselves, appeared. In 1999, Posh Spice married famous footballer David Beckham, went by the name Victoria Beckham and became the face of numerous products and clothes collections, among them Marc Jacobs, Samantha Tavasa, Armani underwear and Roberto Cavalli. In 2005, she created the brand VB Rocks for a line of jeans and in 2006, founded with her husband the brand DVB style for the production of jeans and perfumes. In 2007 she published *That Extra Half an Inch: Hair, Heels and Everything In Between*, a handbook containing fashion and beauty tips.

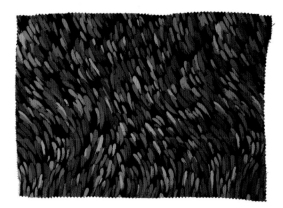

Crepé de chine and silk Georgette,
© Setarium, Educational Silk Museum, Como,
1990s

was based, the mastery in artistic craftsmanship and the search for good taste and design, began to show signs of crisis. This was due especially to the competition of numerous brands that in the meantime had established a place for themselves in the international fashion firmament and consolidated their empires with very effective financial, marketing and advertising strategies.

Mainly French high-end luxury goods sold at exorbitant prices by traditionally famous brands were produced in limited quantities. Mid-range luxury items represented the simplification of high-end products to a semi-industrial format, always at high prices, and constituted a mainly Italian pret à porter. The third level – accessible luxury – included mass-produced products with a carefully studied quality-price relationship. In reality, the frontiers between these categories were being diluted, and designers oriented their creations to the tastes of consumers most loyal to the quality of the collective imagery of the product, offered at competitive prices. "Second signed lines" appeared, and complementary lines of accessories and cosmetics and more economical products that represented the philosophy of the brand but specialised in a specific aspect of their overall identity proliferated. In the market, many types of consumers identified by analysts had become more individualised, and products, increasingly studied, sought to satisfy the needs and aspirations of each one. Specific forms changed quickly, mixing in unheard of and contradictory combinations: much attention was paid to sports, technical materials, experimental fibres and fabrics that provided special benefits. The brand was no longer sufficient to attract possible buyers with the promise of granting them status, something which in the past had served to ensure that consumers would buy things solely for the pleasure of showing them off to others.

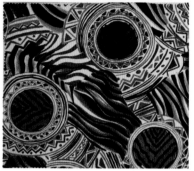

Above right: © Setarium, Educational Silk Museum, Como, 1990s

ICONS OF ELEGANCE: DIANA OF ENGLAND

The modern elegance of the 90s is identified with the unfortunate Princess Diana, catapulted from the peaceful English countryside into the urban spotlight under the curious eyes of the public after her marriage (1981) to Charles of England, heir to the English throne and dedicated to other interests and passions.

Diana embodied with class and poise an "ugly duckling to swan" metamorphosis, attempting to adapt her image, for two decades, to the role that she had been given in life. Fashion was one of her greatest passions, and the things she wore did not always seem appropriate to the stiff British monarchy. However, she quickly became a frame of reference for all ordinary women who identified with her "unhappy fairy tale" life and viewed her as a true heroine of their time.

Third Millenium...
And History Marches On

2000–2015: FASHION, MARKET, COMMUNICATION AND SYTLES

Vivienne Westwood, A/W 2011-2012

At the end of the 20th century, interest grew in dress style as a contemporary phenomenon of communication between the individual and the community. Its natural symbolic language in relation to the formation of identity and communication theory had already been addressed by scholars such as Roland Barthes (*The Fashion System*, 1967), Gilles Lipovetsky (*The Empire of Fashion*, 1989), Gillo Dorfles (*Mode & Modi*, 1979 and *La Moda Della Moda*, 1984) and Ugo Volli (*Contro La Moda*, 1990). After the fall of the Twin Towers (2001), the world's perception changed in a climate of general uncertainty that dominated international markets and insinuated itself into homes and families. With the decline of overarching ideologies, useful in maintaining socioeconomic balance, the psycho-emotional needs of the individual struggled to find acceptance and security. Information became decisive.

COMMUNICATION THROUGH IMAGES

In the post-modern period, image worship was already widespread: *seeming* was more important than *being*. The representations of the self acquired more importance in a social system that oscillated between imitation and identification, homogenization and differentiation, luxury and democracy. One's personal wardrobe was the ideal instrument for interpreting the metaphor of an identity under construction. The "liquid society" of Zygmunt Bauman, which underscored the absence of any solid reference and contained both nostalgia for a lost past and the desire for a technological future, took form. New specialised magazines appeared: *Mood* (2000), *Collezioni Donna* (devoted to prêt-à-porter), *Flair* (2003), *Muse Magazine* (2005), *Velvet* (2006) and *Mug* (2011) suggested but did not impose trends and behavioural models personified in the fashionable elites of the international *jet set* and luminaries of the music and film world. Already existing styles renewed their influence with the help of journalists that experimented with new post-production software. Alexander Liberman, director of *Vogue*, defined fashion photography as "a subtle and complex operation that requires art, talent, technique, psychology and sales ability." The mass media granted increasingly more importance to the fashion sector, with in-depth analysis, fashion shows and interviews with designers. The most innovative international fashion illustrators at that time were Kichisaburo Ogawa, Glenn Tunstull, Bil Donovan, Carlos Aponte and Steven Stipelman. The History of Fashion became a subject of

Jean Paul Gaultier, S/S 2008

Christian Lacroix, S/S 2008

Previous page: Capucci design, homage to Giorginiin the 50th anniversary of Italian fashion, 2001

study at academies, polytechnic schools and specialisation courses in computer science. Fashion was now no longer the exclusive luxury of a select few but a playful tool for reshaping society through the customs, attitudes, forms and content of everyday existence.

POINT OF SALE

The success of chemical technology made the organized production of garments more streamlined and simple through the use of innovative materials in terms of performance (anti-bacteria, anti-stain, anti-wrinkle, anti-wind, extendible, non-deformable, vitaminised, breathable, slimming and perfumed fabrics). However, it also imposed the rules of big finance in billing and redistribution of profits. Companies in the textile and garments sector already established in European markets diversified their investments in more product sectors, were listed on the stock exchange, followed the trend of subcontracting production in countries where the cost of labour is cheaper and privileged a large-scale commercial expansion in southeast Asia, Australia, Saudi Arabia, Russia and other emerging countries. Fashion lost its Eurocentric character and became globalised. All business activity revolved around the point of sale, the cornerstone link between supply and demand. The design of the stores was entrusted to renowned architects. The undisputed protagonist of these changes was Miuccia Prada, who, moving beyond a store's traditional functions, created epicentres of encounters and cultural experimentation that embodied the philosophy and style of the brand: New York (2001, Rem Koolhaas and OMA), Tokyo (2003, Herzog & de Meuron), Los Angeles (2004, Rem Koolhaas and OMA). Other international brands soon adapted to the fashion-design-architecture alliance. In Milan, Corso Como 10, a multifunctional space for experiencing fashion in a new way, appeared. Everything was carefully studied based on the geometry of the spaces, lighting, inventory and mobility in the store's interior, which defined the way in which the customer engaged with the product, extending the amount of time that customers remain in the store. In addition to clothes, we find a vast array of cosmetic accessories and design and decoration objects. The customer was free to move around in a "transversal habitat" and interact emotionally with it. Elegant showrooms and single-brand boutiques, conceived the 80s and 90s as showcases suited to the personality of the designer, were transformed in a minimalist period into genuine cathedrals for the exhibition of merchandise, with exclusive coffee-shop restaurants, art galleries and areas devoted to well being and entertainment. An essential architecture exalted the product to the utmost and expanded neutral support to provide attractive services that gained the customer's loyalty. In times of crisis, unemployment and diminishing acquisitive power, these phenomena were reflected negatively in the dynamics related to consumption and acquisition of garments, and luxury goods in particular suffered a setback.

THE FASHION INDUSTRY: FAST FASHION AND NICHE PRODUCTS

Among sales, acquisitions and business restructuring by large foreign luxury companies, the Italian fashion industry remains a

Prada - Miu Miu, A/W 2010

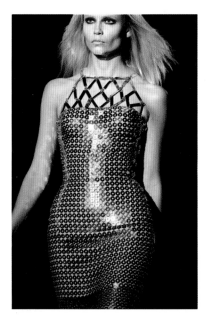

Versace S/S 2013

Valentino HC, S/S 2008

growing phenomenon in the global market panorama. A two-fold scenario emerged that has an influence on the kinds of accessible goods, fast fashion (conceived for a broader range of users) and niche products (aimed at consumer with specific requirements). In the first case, the search for quality is substituted by quantity while variety is defined by the incontestable triumph of the ephemeral. The offer is renewed weekly and includes garments inspired by the fashion runways of the big companies; showcases are a constant lure. Attention is still paid to design, a formal search for perfecting already existing models, always in keeping with the latest trends. The speed at which geographical distances and linguistic and cultural barriers are overcome has become a prevailing value. Large commercial centres have emerged as the main temples of leisure time and consumption. A close connection between the production, distribution and logistic systems allows for reducing the preparation time of collections and responds quickly to market demands. Information on the daily status of sales, including customer opinions, suggestions and requests, results in a beautiful synergy. Interconnected networks heighten the feverish fascination with everything in a constant state of flux such as fashion, perceived as the only constant in the contemporary world. What one wears no longer has a defined style, one that can be labelled within set parameters. In the second case, niche products prevail, separating themselves along a parallel track between fashion and design with clothes as the common denominator. In the search for the recovery of international competitiveness, some brands have rediscovered their manufacturing vocation and now place emphasis on their primordial image, which they update constantly to avoid the trivialisation of the market, while keeping it consistent over time with the unmistakeable characteristics of the brand's inherent style. Combining modernity and history, they seek to present authentic and original fashion to a public that has everything already, which is not easily satisfied and moves from one capital to another, wanting to appear independent and cosmopolitan. The craftsmanship side of sartorial work, which had become increasingly scant and marginal, came to be appreciated again. Custom-made products appeared, created on demand according to the customer's expectations, with personalised colours and materials. Parisian fashion runways have opted for spectacularisation through the visionary and monumental work of John Galliano, Marc Jacob and Alexander McQuinn, although in sales common sense and reasonable wearability prevail.

LOTS OF TRENDS, NO REQUIREMENTS

Since 2000, fashion has become less authoritarian and rediscovered some absolute classics: the camel skin coat, cashmere sweater, three-piece suit, casual moccasins, button-down collar shirt, tight black formal dress, pants suit, blazer, raincoat, to name a few. Along with these classics are more casual and sportier garments such as leggings, sneakers, parkas, jackets with zippers, t-shirts and ankle boots that express a strong desire for freedom. Despite the fact that they embody very different styles, one can look fashionable wearing garments by Armani, Chanel, Comme des Garçons or Dries van Noten. Important commercial phenomena such as Zara and H&M, which have extended throughout the world, represented an exit route from the crisis, suggesting the combination of a brand-name garment with a more economical one and even adding an ethnic or vintage touch.

ETHNIC SUGGESTIONS

Ethnic influences are a testament to the combination of emerging diversified cultures, an intersection of mental itineraries narrated through the exhibitions and fashions shows of designers from countries such as Japan, Brazil, Turkey, Africa and China that have experienced international success. Fashion collections paint a picture of what is looming on the horizon. Fashion designers and "cool hunters" travel continuously and video record whatever catches their eye. Gathering information about how people dress, depending on the place, time and setting, they rework and juxtapose all these data with the trends of the most renowned fashion runways. This research is the basis for the creation of styles.

THE VINTAGE PHENOMENON

The used clothing market, already in vogue in the 70s as a form of youth protest, represents a new source of fascination. Garment production from the 20th century, still accessible in antique markets and personal archives of fashion houses, attracts the curiosity of collectors and sector executives. Important museum institutions collect historic documentation materials and provide fashion with

Dries van Noten, A/W 2010

Chanel, A/W 2010

Armani Privé HC, S/S 2007

Hermes, S/S 2010

exhibition spaces previously confined to art. Vintage garments have become a must in anyone's wardrobe, a distinguishing element thanks to their singularity and rareness within a spectrum of overly homogenous choices. Truly heterogeneous harvests of clothing, some for daily use, such as A.n.g.e.l.o by Angelo Caroli, have become accessible and usable through renting and are widely used as a source of inspiration for new proposals. With the discovery of vintage garments, fashion has reinterpreted its past glory and transferred to the present a deeper cultural and aesthetic inheritance. Prada, Gucci, Vuitton, Ferragamo, Hermes, Chanel and Givenchy faithfully apply brand management to specific product lines and pursue the narration of their history through re-editions of "emblematic designs". The glow of the best designs of the 30s, 40s, 50s, 60s and 70s reappears in kind of remodelling that appropriates details, finishes, buttons, texture design, colours of a print or the arrangement of an accessory. Including a reference constitutes an added value for the contemporary piece of clothing. Garments intended for the youth market are thus subjected to processes of ageing, wear and tear and overdyeing, reconfigured in creative code with cutting-edge technologies.

THE IMPORTANCE OF THE CONSUMER

This general trend establishes the centrality of the consumer. It reinstates consumers by granting them the freedom to dress the way they like, customising styles and adapting them to their needs and to the occasion independently. All codes are subverted and rearranged, to the point that if someone wears only one brand, they are considered out of date. Dress style had been decreed by rules and conventions to underscore national, civil, sexual and professional identity. These strictures, however, were changed by the desire to achieve personal and social expression and the need for legitimation, prominence and even omnipotence when wholly or partially reinterpreting the body.

PHOTOGRAPHERS AND MODELS OF BEHAVIOUR

Alexander McQueen, A/W 2010

After a period of absolute prominence, fashion models are increasingly thin and skeletal. They play a neutral supporting role in which the garments and the designer's talent must prevail. Among the most charismatic is Kate Moss, who has become, despite everything, a true icon of style. The ironic New York photographer Terry Richardson, responsible for controversial fashion campaigns for Gucci, Marc Jacobs, Levi's, Miu Miu, Pirelli, Hugo Boss, Costume National, Tom Ford, Diesel and Tommy Hilfiger did some photo shoots in the "back rooms" of fashion shows, focusing on the work that goes on "behind the scenes" of the dazzling fashion system. Richardson's criticism of certain aspects regarding sex and drugs, up to that time censured, caused a scandal. Another photographer, Oliviero Toscani, active for many years in the Fabrica de Benetton cultural laboratory, undertook a photographic campaign against anorexia, a sickness that afflicts many models obsessed with fasting in order to be able to fit into a boyish size 38.

SUSTAINABILITY AND ECOLOGY

The concern for ecology has awakened people's consciences and oriented the public toward the acquisition of sustainable products. The essay *No Logo* by the Canadian journalist Naomi Klein (2000) analyses the phenomenon of branding and has become a reference text in the anti-globalisation movement. Fashion brands that produce their products through the exploitation of child labour received negative publicity. The theme of Expo 2015 was the sustainability of the planet, and fashion wants to participate as well from the recycling of garments discarded in the H&M campaign to Vivienne Westwood's organic cotton t-shirts; from Armani hemp jeans to Crespi's bamboo fibre garments; from the preference for non-violent silk to accessories made with corn and orange peel that represent an alternative to materials such as silver fibre and Goretex membranes.

THE SUPERMARKET OF STYLES AND FASHION FUSION

Having overcome the usual limits of style, fashion no longer offers certainties, straying from the path of a "single and consistent trend that anyone who wants to be fashionable" must follow. Instead it has adopted what Ted Polhemus has defined as the "supermarket of styles". On the fashion runways of Milan, Paris, London and New York a "fusion style" now prevails. Diverse trends co-exist, intersecting and combining with each other in hybrid designs capable of revolutionising rigid styles and canonical rules, essential pillars of any characterisation of the times.

NEW FASHION PROFESSIONALS

The combination of rules reflects the need to shock and obtain the consensus of journalists and consumers. Increasingly, recourse is made to a new professional figure – the stylist – who combines, coordinates and mixes entire garment collections – specifically created by fashion designers, enveloping them in mystery and captivating fascination under their rigorous and confident direction. As a result, fashion personifies thousands of lives, a multitude of collective aspirations, especially those of people who are unable to find satisfaction or realisation in other areas. It has become a kind of swelling of styles, a loss of authority of the control mechanism over fashion by the production system while the consumption of objects is conveyed primarily through advertising and the media, which stimulate the innermost motivations, unconscious or voluntary, of humanity as a whole. Fashion bloggers are responsible for the latest trend, which subverts stereotypes and points toward complete democratization. From websites created for this purpose, they comment on the garments worn by famous people and express preferences for the inspirations of the latest fashion shows or street trends. In a casual and ironic tone, they share their thoughts on the Internet about fashion, beauty and quality of life and in the process have become the new gurus of contemporary taste.

Dolce & Gabbana, "Hymn to maternity",
A/W 2015-16

INDEX

Karl Lagerfeld against war and in favour of women's rights, A/W 2014-2015

"Fashion not something that exists in dresses only. Fashion is in the sky, in the street, fashion has to do with ideas, the way we live, what is happening"

COCO CHANEL